QUANTUM KIDDIES

Kids Activity Books
Ages 8-12 | Vol -1 | Fractions

ActivityCrusades

Published by Speedy Publishing Canada Limited

ActivityCrusades
activity books

FRACTIONS

Write the fraction of the shaded part.

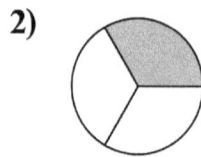

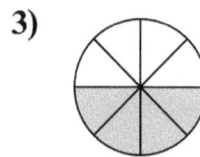

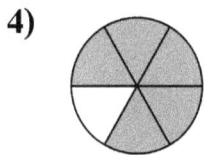

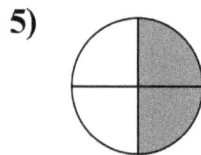

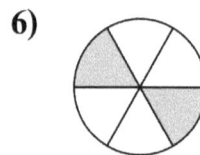

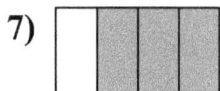

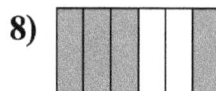

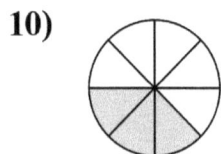

1)

2)

3)

4)

5)

6)

7)

8)

9)

10)

Ex. **²/₈**

1. _____

2. _____

3. _____

4. _____

5. _____

6. _____

7. _____

8. _____

9. _____

10. _____

1)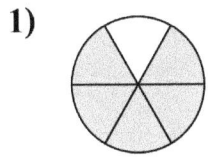

2)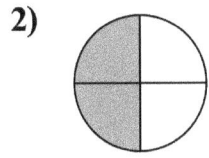

3)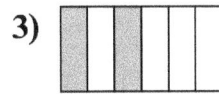

4)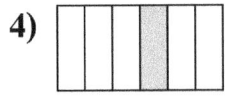

5)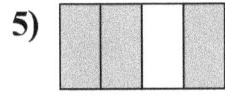

6)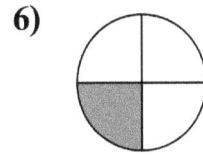

7)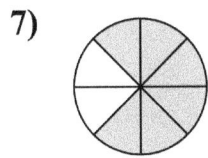

8)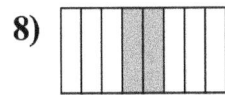

9)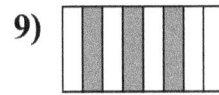

10)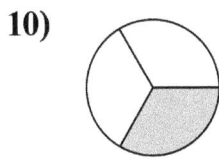

1. _____

2. _____

3. _____

4. _____

5. _____

6. _____

7. _____

8. _____

9. _____

10. _____

1)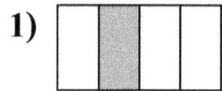

2)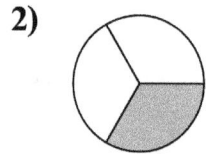

3)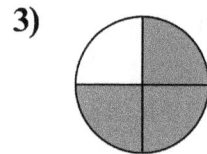

4)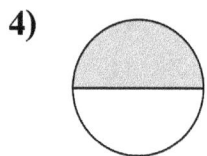

5)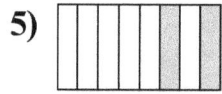

6)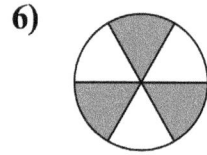

7)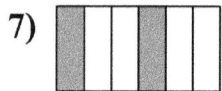

8)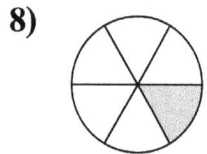

9)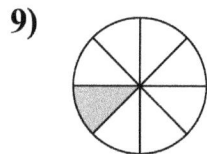

10)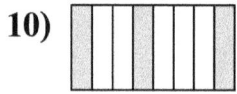

1. _____

2. _____

3. _____

4. _____

5. _____

6. _____

7. _____

8. _____

9. _____

10. _____

1)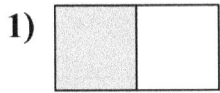

2)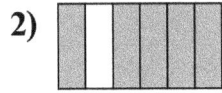

3)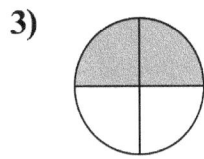

4)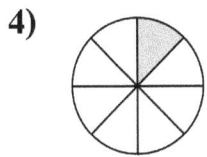

5)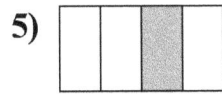

6)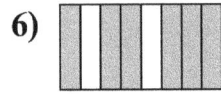

7)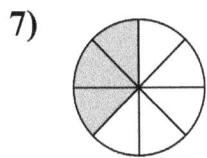

8)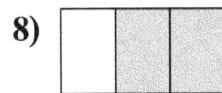

9)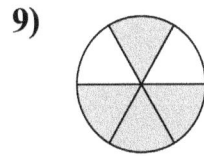

10)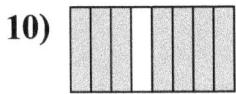

1. _____

2. _____

3. _____

4. _____

5. _____

6. _____

7. _____

8. _____

9. _____

10. _____

1)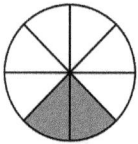

2)

3)

4)

5)

6)

7)

8)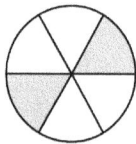

9)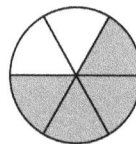

10)

1. _____

2. _____

3. _____

4. _____

5. _____

6. _____

7. _____

8. _____

9. _____

10. _____

1)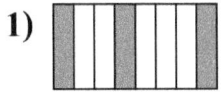

2)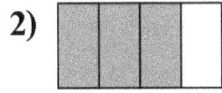

3)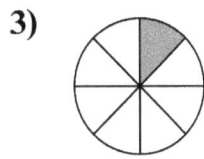

4)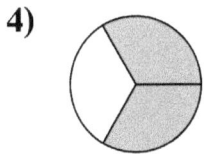

5)

6)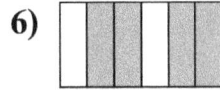

7)

8)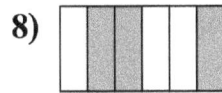

9)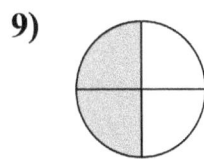

10)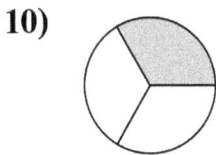

1. _____

2. _____

3. _____

4. _____

5. _____

6. _____

7. _____

8. _____

9. _____

10. _____

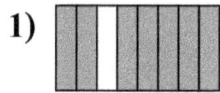

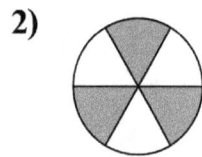

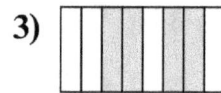

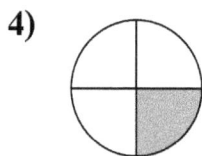

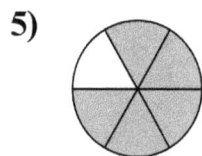

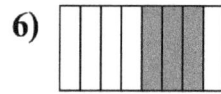

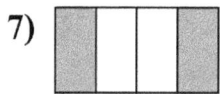

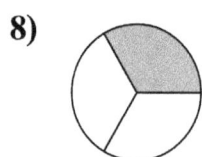

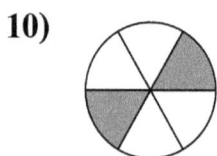

1)

2)

3)

4)

5)

6)

7)

8)

9)

10)

1. _____

2. _____

3. _____

4. _____

5. _____

6. _____

7. _____

8. _____

9. _____

10. _____

8

1)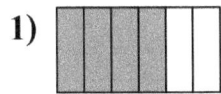

2)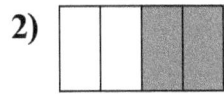

3)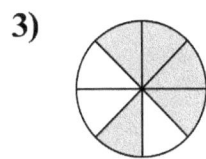

4)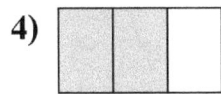

5)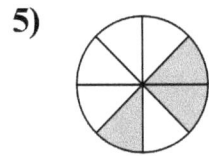

6)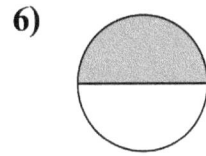

7)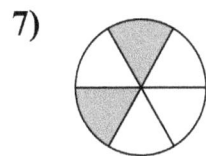

8)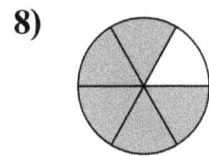

9)

10)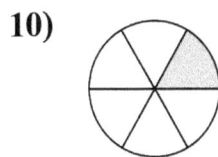

1. _____
2. _____
3. _____
4. _____
5. _____
6. _____
7. _____
8. _____
9. _____
10. _____

1)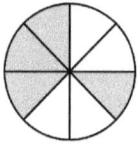

2)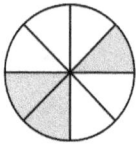

3)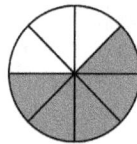

4)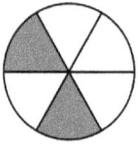

5)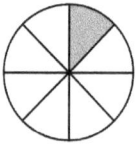

6)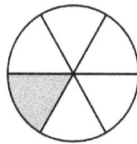

7)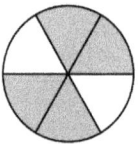

8)

9)

10)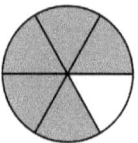

1. _____

2. _____

3. _____

4. _____

5. _____

6. _____

7. _____

8. _____

9. _____

10. _____

1)

2)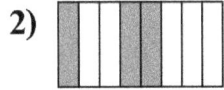

3)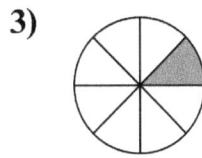

4)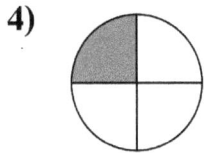

5)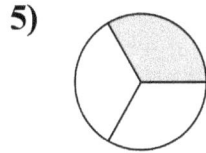

6)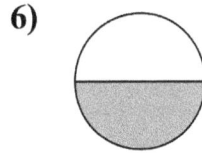

7)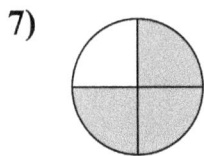

8)

9)

10)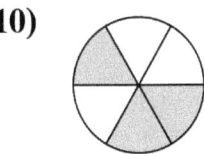

1. _____

2. _____

3. _____

4. _____

5. _____

6. _____

7. _____

8. _____

9. _____

10. _____

Determine which choice(s) show the shape partitioned so each piece has equal area. If none, write 'none'.

1) A.  B. ▭ C. ▯ D. ◹

2) A. ▷ B. △ C. ▽ D. ▥

3) A. ✦ B. ◁ C. ⊖ D. ▦

4) A. ◍ B. ✳ C. △ D. ◁

5) A. ⬡ B. ✳ C. ✦ D. ⬡

6) A. ⬠ B. ⬠ C. ◁ D. ⯃

7) A. ✫ B. ⊙ C. ◁ D. ⬠

8) A. ⬡ B. ⊕ C. ✦ D. ✧

Ex.

1. __A, B, D__

2. _____

3. _____

4. _____

5. _____

6. _____

7. _____

8. _____

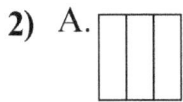

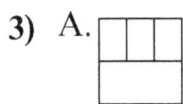

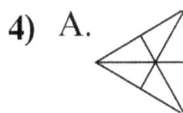

1) A. B. C. D.

2) A. B. C. D.

3) A. B. C. D.

4) A. B. C. D.

5) A. B. C. D.

6) A. B. C. D.

7) A. B. C. D.

8) A. B. C. D.

1. _____
2. _____
3. _____
4. _____
5. _____
6. _____
7. _____
8. _____

1) A. 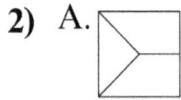   B. ⬤   C. ◻   D. ◻

2) A. ◻   B. ⬤   C. ▷   D. ◻

3) A. ⬤   B. ◻   C. ▷   D. ◻

4) A. ▽   B. ▽   C. ⬤   D. ⬤

5) A. ⬤   B. ⬡   C. ⬡   D. △

6) A. ⬠   B. ⬡   C. ★   D. ✦

7) A. △   B. ★   C. ✦   D. ⬭

8) A. ✦   B. ★   C. ◻   D. ⬡

1. _____
2. _____
3. _____
4. _____
5. _____
6. _____
7. _____
8. _____

1) A. 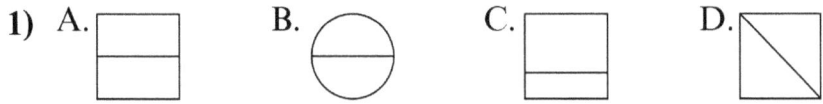 B. C. D.

2) A. 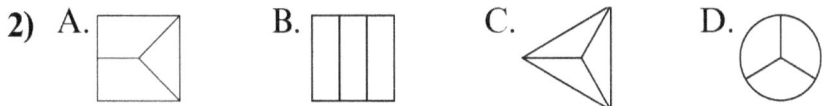 B. C. D.

3) A.  B. C. D.

4) A.  B. C. D.

5) A.  B. C. D.

6) A.  B. C. D.

7) A.  B. C. D.

8) A.  B. C. D.

1. _____

2. _____

3. _____

4. _____

5. _____

6. _____

7. _____

8. _____

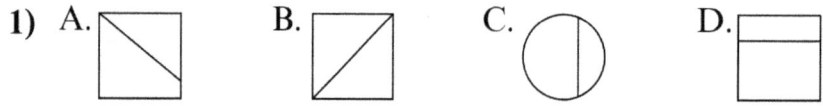

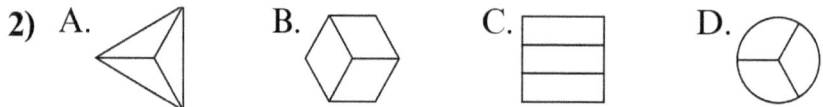

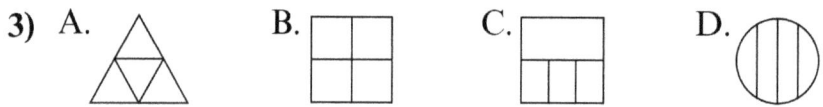

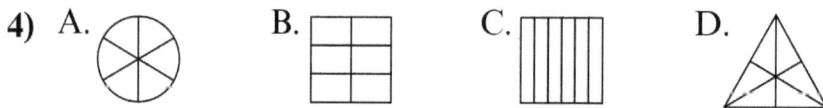

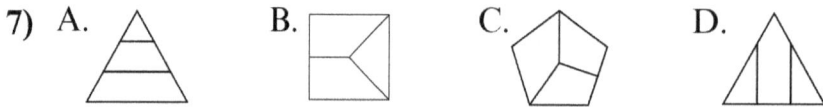

1) A.   B.   C.   D.

2) A.   B.   C.   D.

3) A.   B.   C.   D.

4) A.   B.   C.   D.

5) A.   B.   C.   D.

6) A.   B.   C.   D.

7) A.   B.   C.   D.

8) A.   B.   C.   D.

1. _____
2. _____
3. _____
4. _____
5. _____
6. _____
7. _____
8. _____

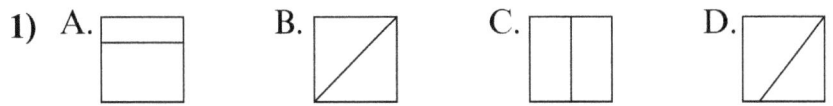

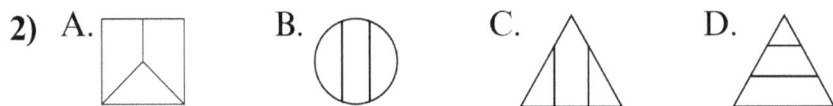

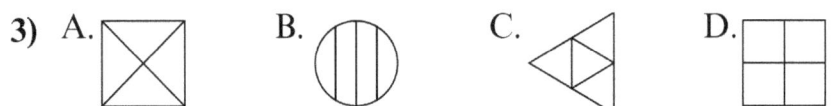

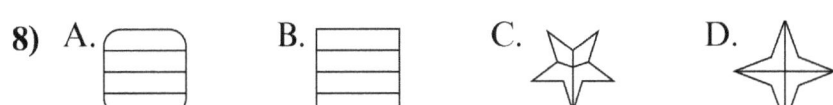

1) A.   B.   C.   D.

2) A.   B.   C.   D.

3) A.   B.   C.   D.

4) A.   B.   C.   D.

5) A.   B.   C.   D.

6) A.   B.   C.   D.

7) A.   B.   C.   D.

8) A.   B.   C.   D.

1. _____
2. _____
3. _____
4. _____
5. _____
6. _____
7. _____
8. _____

1) A. 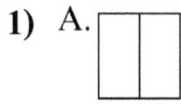 B. C. D.

2) A. 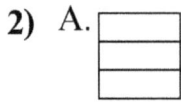 B. C. D.

3) A.  B. C. D.

4) A.  B. C. D.

5) A. 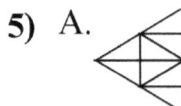 B. C. D.

6) A.  B. C. D.

7) A.  B. C. D.

8) A. 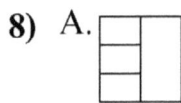 B. C. D.

1. _____

2. _____

3. _____

4. _____

5. _____

6. _____

7. _____

8. _____

1) A.  B. C. D.

2) A. 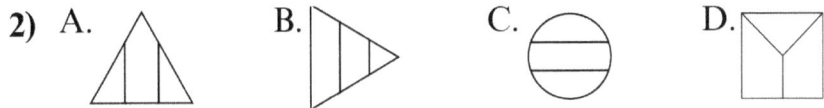 B. C. D.

3) A.  B. C. D.

4) A. 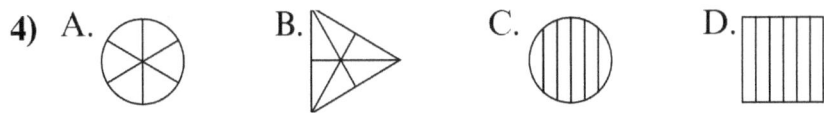 B. C. D.

5) A. 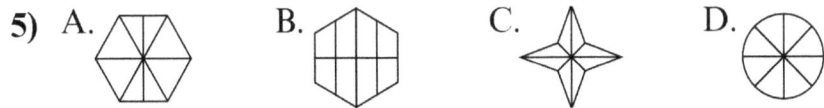 B. C. D.

6) A.  B. C. D.

7) A. 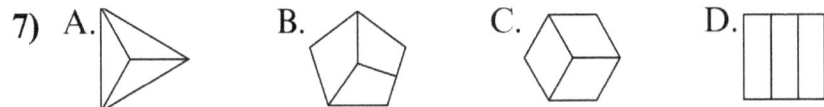 B. C. D.

8) A.  B. C. D.

1. _____

2. _____

3. _____

4. _____

5. _____

6. _____

7. _____

8. _____

1)   A.   B.   C.   D.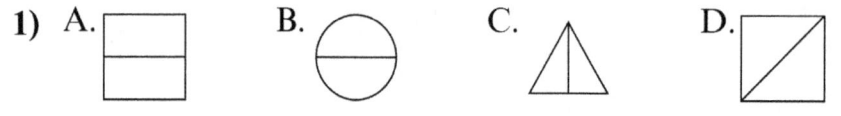

2)   A.   B.   C.   D.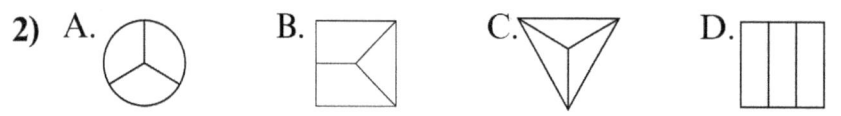

3)   A.   B.   C.   D.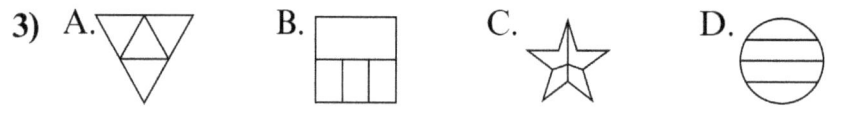

4)   A.   B.   C.   D.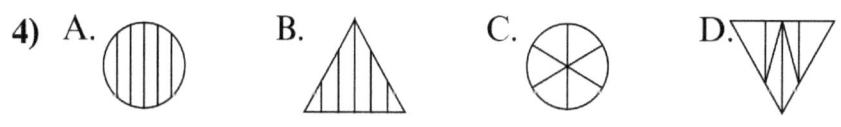

5)   A.   B.   C.   D.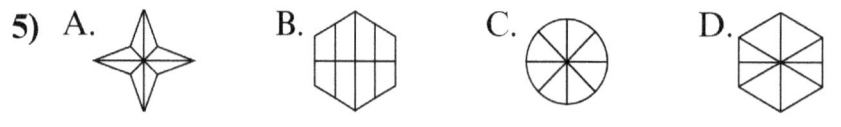

6)   A.   B.   C.   D.

7)   A.   B.   C.   D.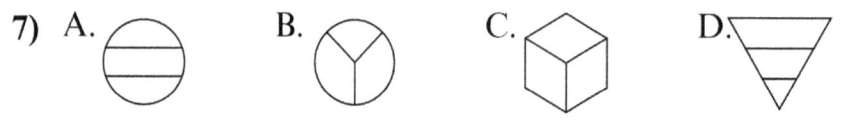

8)   A.   B.   C.   D.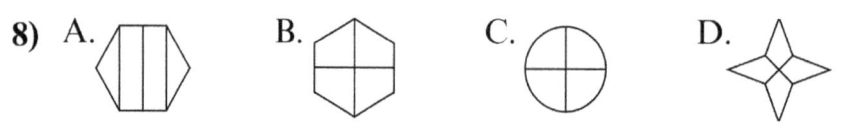

1. _____
2. _____
3. _____
4. _____
5. _____
6. _____
7. _____
8. _____

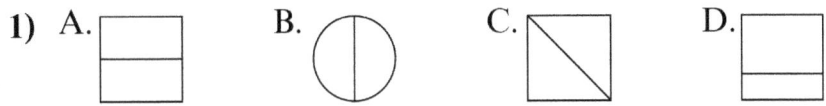

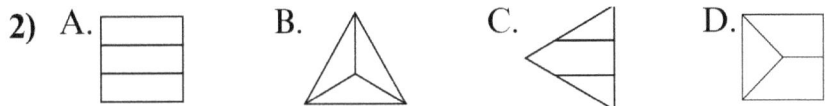

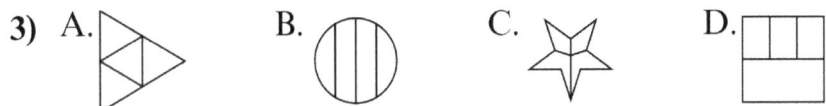

1) A. B. C. D.

2) A. B. C. D.

3) A. B. C. D.

4) A. B. C. D.

5) A. B. C. D.

6) A. B. C. D.

7) A. B. C. D.

8) A. B. C. D.

1. _____
2. _____
3. _____
4. _____
5. _____
6. _____
7. _____
8. _____

Shade in the fraction to solve the problem.

Ex.

1)

2)

3)

4)

5)

6)

7)

8)

9)

10)

Ex. $\dfrac{3}{7} + \dfrac{2}{7} = \dfrac{5}{7}$

1. ___ + ___ = ___

2. ___ + ___ = ___

3. ___ + ___ = ___

4. ___ + ___ = ___

5. ___ + ___ = ___

6. ___ + ___ = ___

7. ___ + ___ = ___

8. ___ + ___ = ___

9. ___ + ___ = ___

10. ___ + ___ = ___

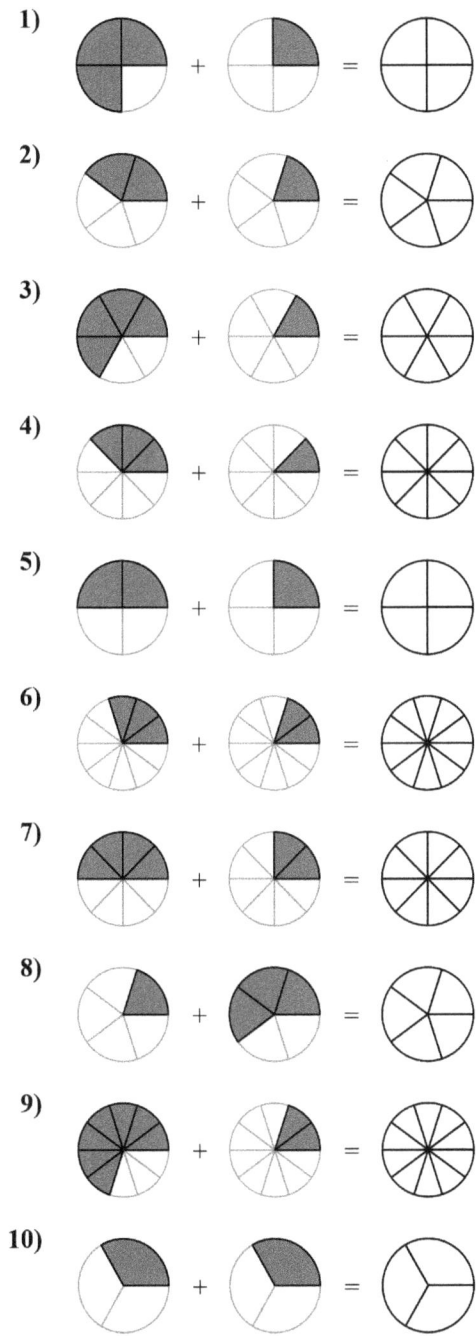

1)

2)

3)

4)

5)

6)

7)

8)

9)

10)

1. ___ + ___ = ___

2. ___ + ___ = ___

3. ___ + ___ = ___

4. ___ + ___ = ___

5. ___ + ___ = ___

6. ___ + ___ = ___

7. ___ + ___ = ___

8. ___ + ___ = ___

9. ___ + ___ = ___

10. ___ + ___ = ___

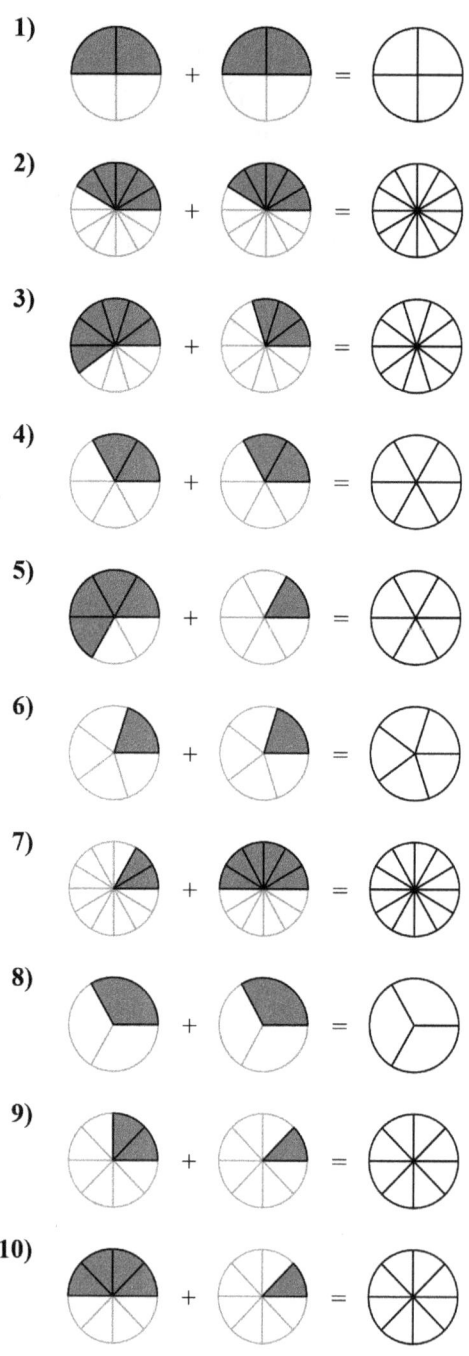

1)

2)

3)

4)

5)

6)

7)

8)

9)

10)

1. ___ + ___ = ___

2. ___ + ___ = ___

3. ___ + ___ = ___

4. ___ + ___ = ___

5. ___ + ___ = ___

6. ___ + ___ = ___

7. ___ + ___ = ___

8. ___ + ___ = ___

9. ___ + ___ = ___

10. ___ + ___ = ___

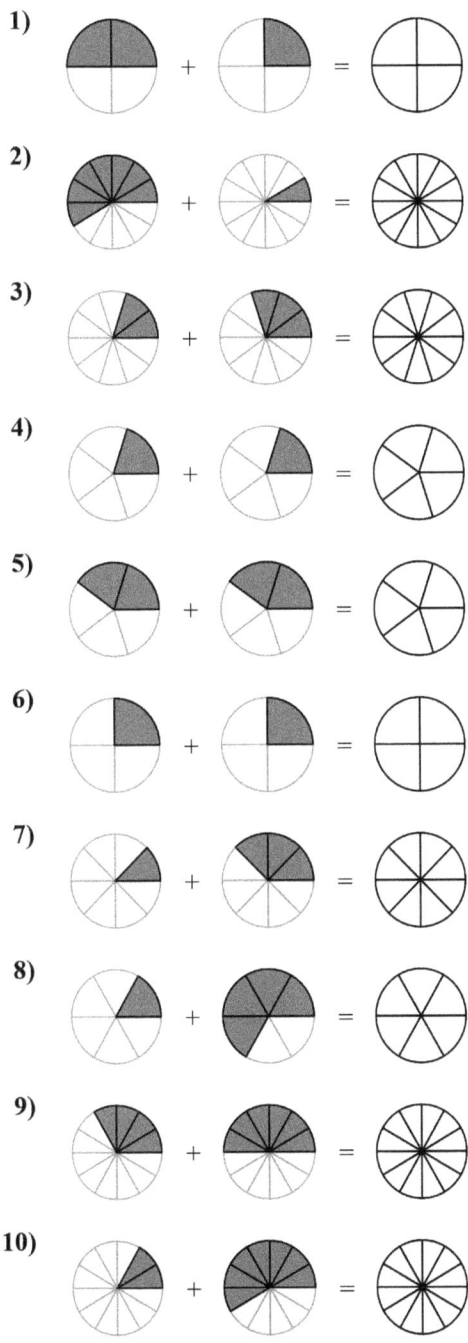

24

1)

2)

3)

4)

5)

6)

7)

8)

9)

10)

1. ___ + ___ = ___

2. ___ + ___ = ___

3. ___ + ___ = ___

4. ___ + ___ = ___

5. ___ + ___ = ___

6. ___ + ___ = ___

7. ___ + ___ = ___

8. ___ + ___ = ___

9. ___ + ___ = ___

10. ___ + ___ = ___

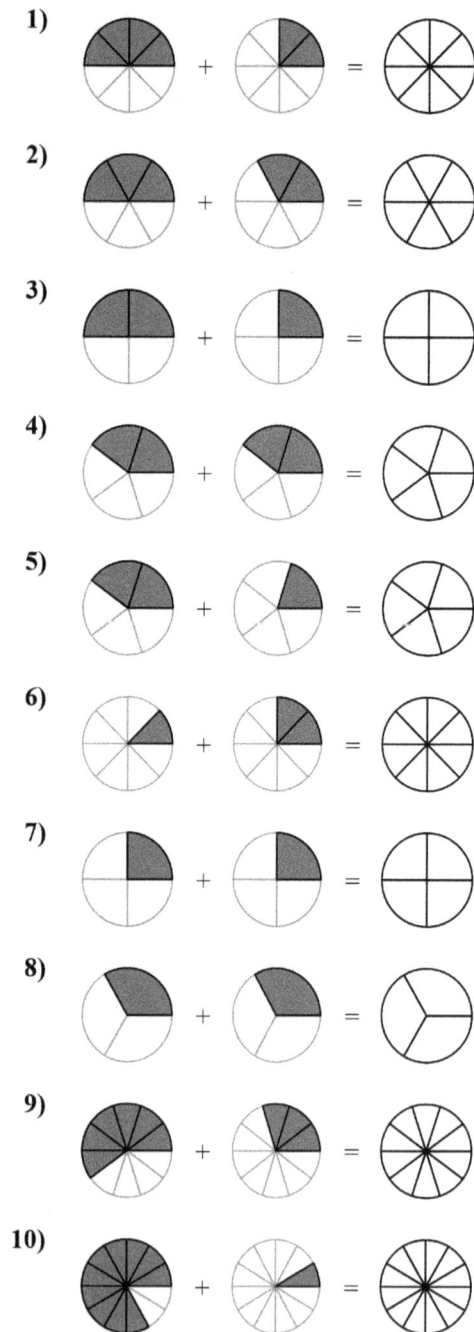

1) + =

2) + =

3) + =

4) + =

5) + =

6) + =

7) + =

8) + =

9) + =

10) + =

1. ___ + ___ = ___

2. ___ + ___ = ___

3. ___ + ___ = ___

4. ___ + ___ = ___

5. ___ + ___ = ___

6. ___ + ___ = ___

7. ___ + ___ = ___

8. ___ + ___ = ___

9. ___ + ___ = ___

10. ___ + ___ = ___

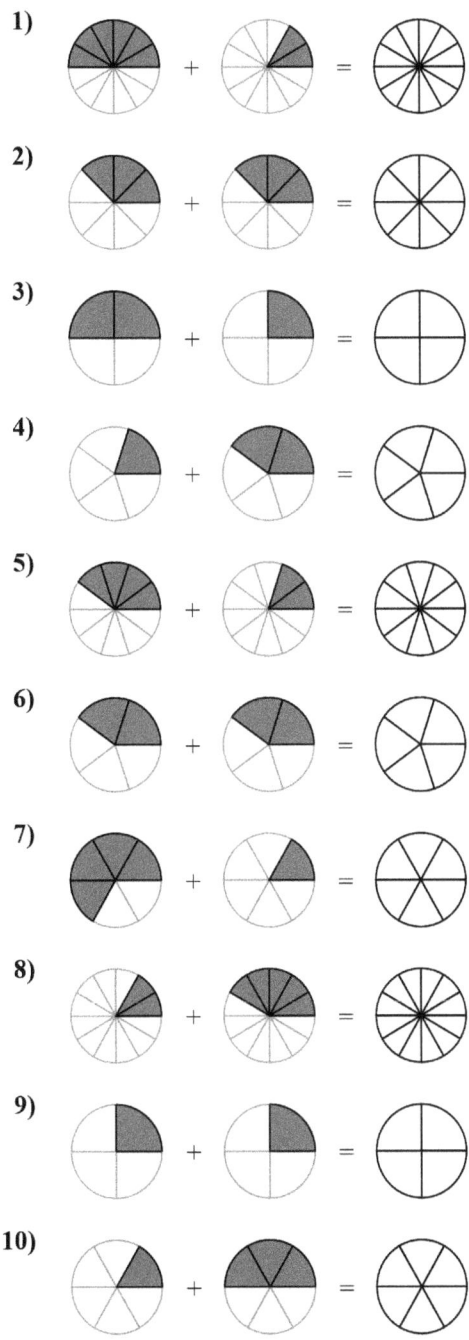

26

1)

2)

3)

4)

5)

6)

7)

8)

9)

10)

1. ___ + ___ = ___

2. ___ + ___ = ___

3. ___ + ___ = ___

4. ___ + ___ = ___

5. ___ + ___ = ___

6. ___ + ___ = ___

7. ___ + ___ = ___

8. ___ + ___ = ___

9. ___ + ___ = ___

10. ___ + ___ = ___

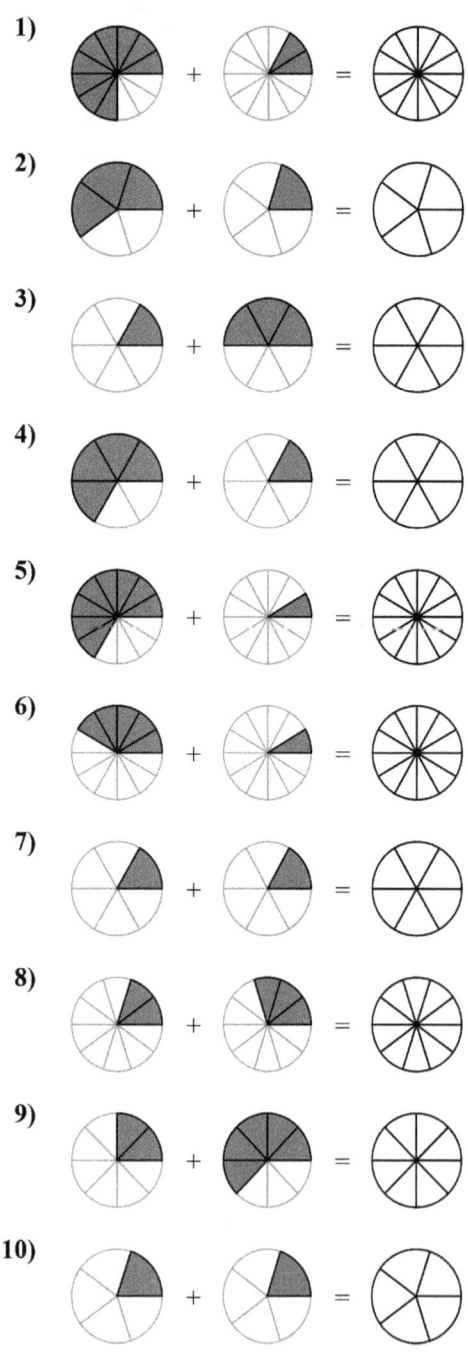

1)

2)

3)

4)

5)

6)

7)

8)

9)

10)

1. ___ + ___ = ___

2. ___ + ___ = ___

3. ___ + ___ = ___

4. ___ + ___ = ___

5. ___ + ___ = ___

6. ___ + ___ = ___

7. ___ + ___ = ___

8. ___ + ___ = ___

9. ___ + ___ = ___

10. ___ + ___ = ___

1)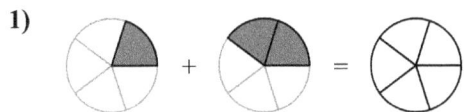

2)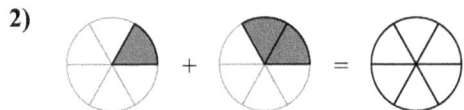

3)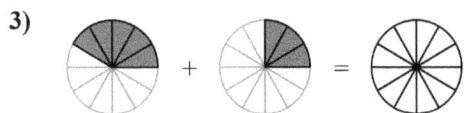

4)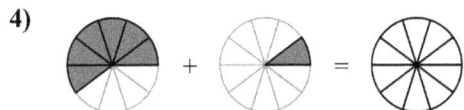

5)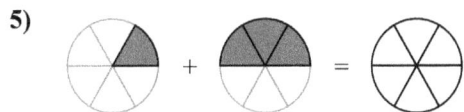

6)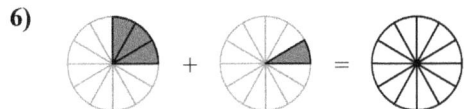

7)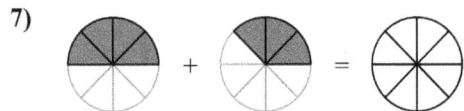

8)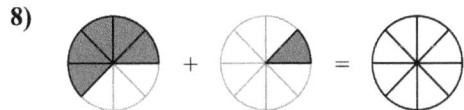

9)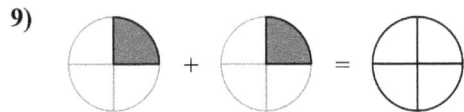

10)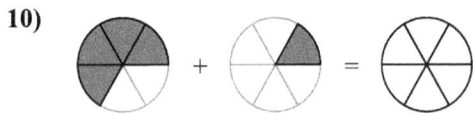

1. ___ + ___ = ___

2. ___ + ___ = ___

3. ___ + ___ = ___

4. ___ + ___ = ___

5. ___ + ___ = ___

6. ___ + ___ = ___

7. ___ + ___ = ___

8. ___ + ___ = ___

9. ___ + ___ = ___

10. ___ + ___ = ___

1)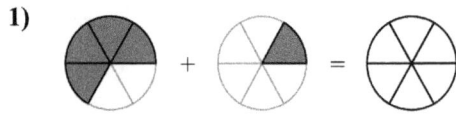

2)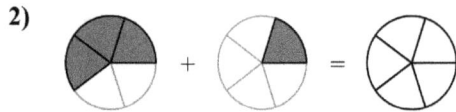

3)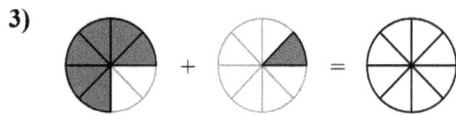

4)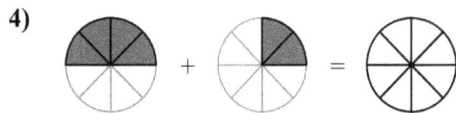

5)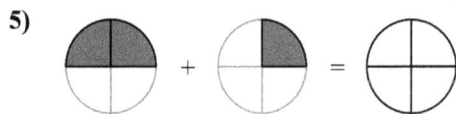

6)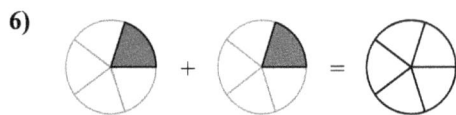

7)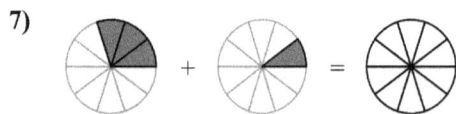

8)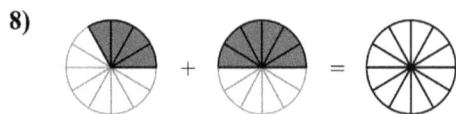

9)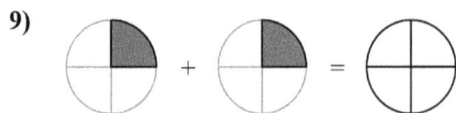

10)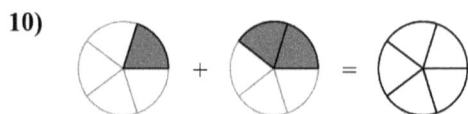

1. ____ + ____ = ____

2. ____ + ____ = ____

3. ____ + ____ = ____

4. ____ + ____ = ____

5. ____ + ____ = ____

6. ____ + ____ = ____

7. ____ + ____ = ____

8. ____ + ____ = ____

9. ____ + ____ = ____

10. ____ + ____ = ____

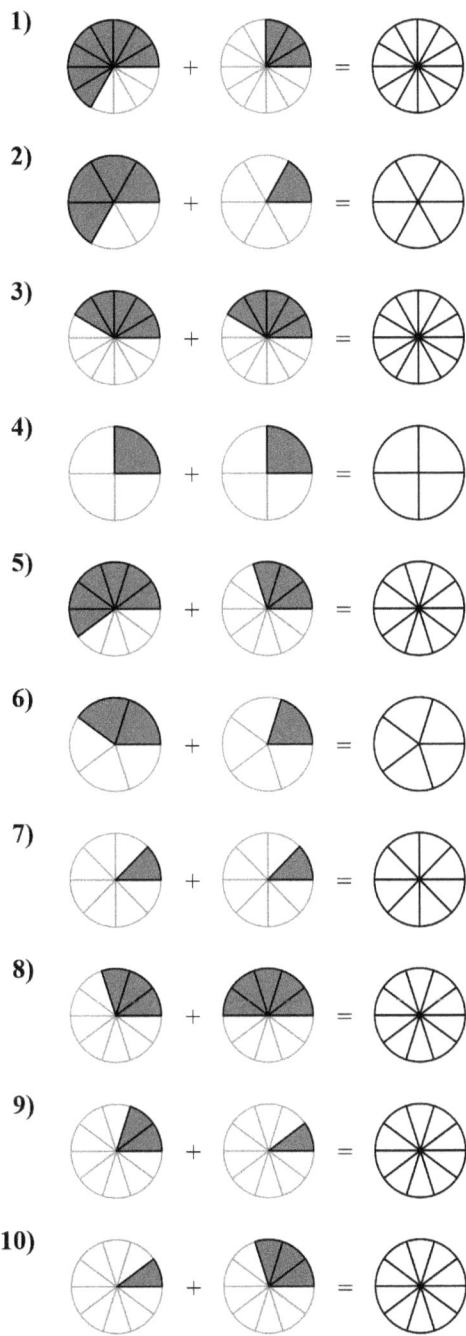

1)

2)

3)

4)

5)

6)

7)

8)

9)

10)

1. ___ + ___ = ___

2. ___ + ___ = ___

3. ___ + ___ = ___

4. ___ + ___ = ___

5. ___ + ___ = ___

6. ___ + ___ = ___

7. ___ + ___ = ___

8. ___ + ___ = ___

9. ___ + ___ = ___

10. ___ + ___ = ___

Use the visual models to solve.

Ex.

1) $\frac{1}{2} \times 7 =$

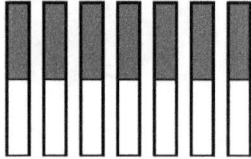

2) $\frac{1}{5} \times 2 =$

3) $\frac{1}{3} \times 5 =$

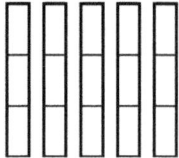

4) $\frac{1}{2} \times 5 =$

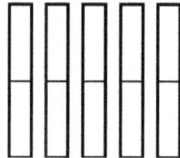

5) $\frac{3}{4} \times 4 =$

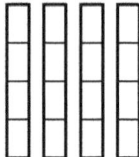

6) $\frac{3}{8} \times 7 =$

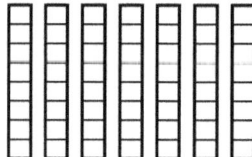

7) $\frac{2}{6} \times 3 =$

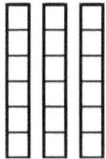

8) $\frac{1}{2} \times 5 =$

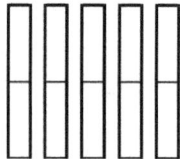

9) $\frac{1}{2} \times 5 =$

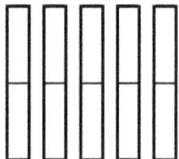

10) $\frac{3}{5} \times 5 =$

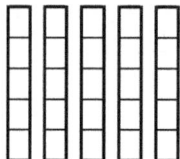

Ex. $\dfrac{7}{2}$

1. _____

2. _____

3. _____

4. _____

5. _____

6. _____

7. _____

8. _____

9. _____

10. _____

1) $\frac{1}{4} \times 9 =$

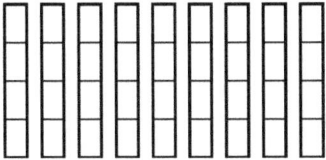

2) $\frac{1}{4} \times 7 =$

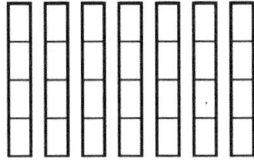

3) $\frac{3}{5} \times 6 =$

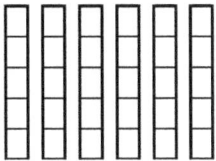

4) $\frac{9}{10} \times 2 =$

5) $\frac{1}{5} \times 4 =$

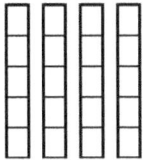

6) $\frac{3}{5} \times 8 =$

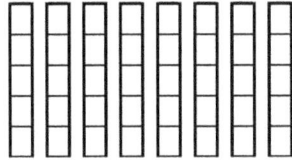

7) $\frac{1}{2} \times 8 =$

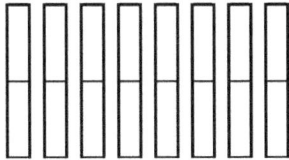

8) $\frac{2}{4} \times 4 =$

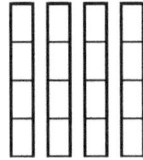

9) $\frac{2}{4} \times 2 =$

10) $\frac{6}{8} \times 2 =$

1. _____

2. _____

3. _____

4. _____

5. _____

6. _____

7. _____

8. _____

9. _____

10. _____

33

1) $\frac{9}{10} \times 6 =$

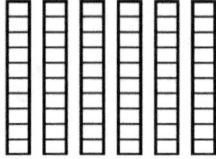

2) $\frac{7}{8} \times 7 =$

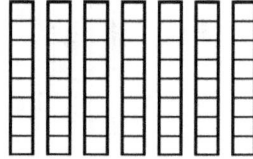

3) $\frac{2}{3} \times 4 =$

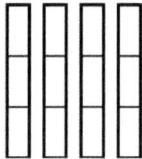

4) $\frac{5}{6} \times 5 =$

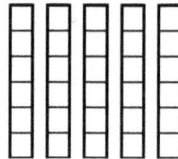

5) $\frac{2}{3} \times 5 =$

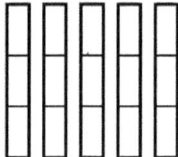

6) $\frac{1}{8} \times 5 =$

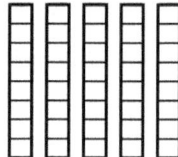

7) $\frac{9}{10} \times 8 =$

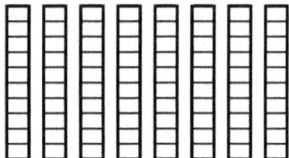

8) $\frac{2}{8} \times 9 =$

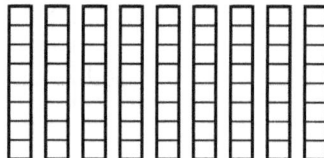

9) $\frac{3}{5} \times 4 =$

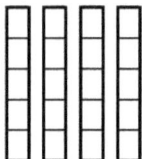

10) $\frac{2}{4} \times 7 =$

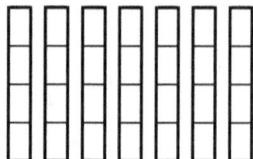

1. _____
2. _____
3. _____
4. _____
5. _____
6. _____
7. _____
8. _____
9. _____
10. _____

1) $\frac{2}{3} \times 9 =$

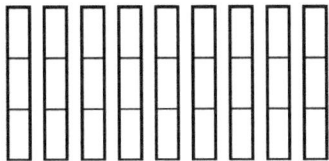

2) $\frac{7}{10} \times 7 =$

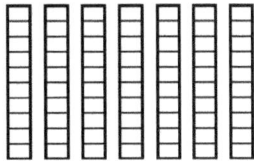

3) $\frac{6}{10} \times 2 =$

4) $\frac{2}{3} \times 7 =$

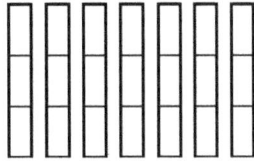

5) $\frac{1}{3} \times 5 =$

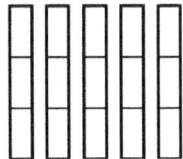

6) $\frac{2}{8} \times 7 =$

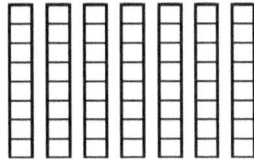

7) $\frac{2}{5} \times 9 =$

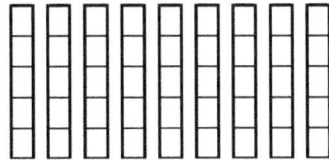

8) $\frac{1}{3} \times 3 =$

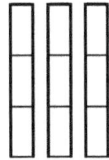

9) $\frac{1}{2} \times 5 =$

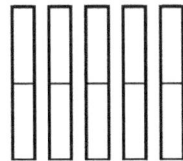

10) $\frac{3}{4} \times 9 =$

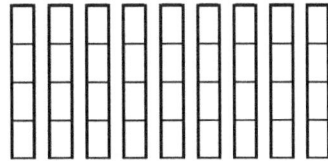

1. _____
2. _____
3. _____
4. _____
5. _____
6. _____
7. _____
8. _____
9. _____
10. _____

1) $\frac{1}{4} \times 7 =$

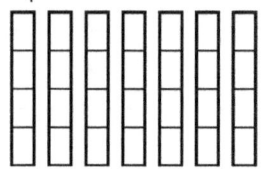

2) $\frac{6}{8} \times 9 =$

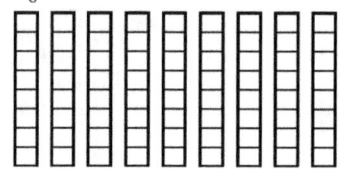

3) $\frac{7}{8} \times 3 =$

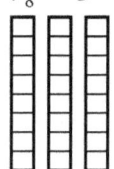

4) $\frac{2}{6} \times 9 =$

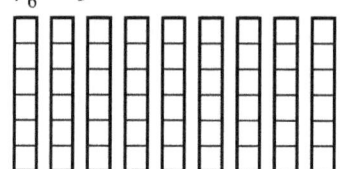

5) $\frac{1}{2} \times 9 =$

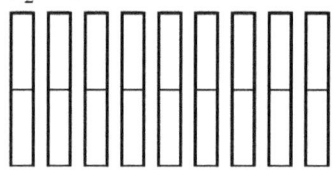

6) $\frac{1}{3} \times 6 =$

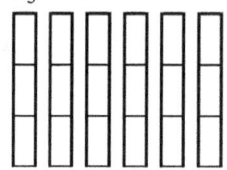

7) $\frac{1}{8} \times 3 =$

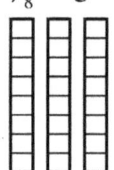

8) $\frac{2}{5} \times 5 =$

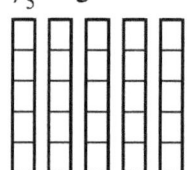

9) $\frac{5}{6} \times 4 =$

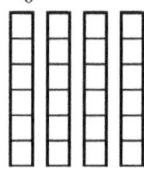

10) $\frac{1}{2} \times 6 =$

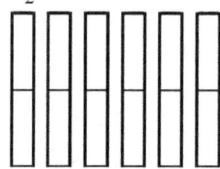

1. _____

2. _____

3. _____

4. _____

5. _____

6. _____

7. _____

8. _____

9. _____

10. _____

1) $\frac{5}{6} \times 5 =$

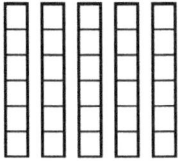

2) $\frac{2}{6} \times 8 =$

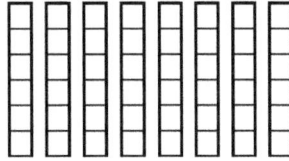

3) $\frac{5}{6} \times 5 =$

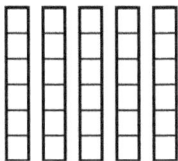

4) $\frac{1}{2} \times 6 =$

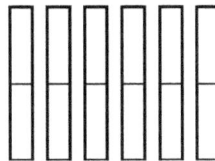

5) $\frac{2}{6} \times 9 =$

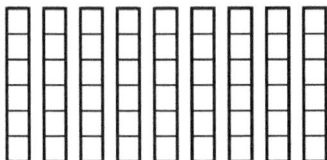

6) $\frac{2}{3} \times 3 =$

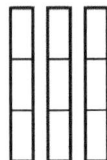

7) $\frac{2}{3} \times 5 =$

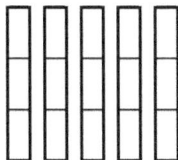

8) $\frac{3}{4} \times 3 =$

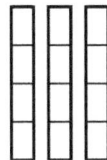

9) $\frac{5}{10} \times 3 =$

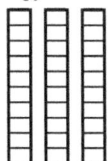

10) $\frac{3}{6} \times 8 =$

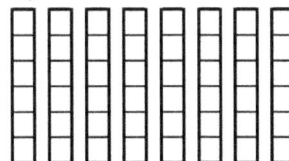

1. _____
2. _____
3. _____
4. _____
5. _____
6. _____
7. _____
8. _____
9. _____
10. _____

1) $\frac{1}{2} \times 4 =$

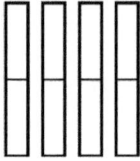

2) $\frac{1}{5} \times 8 =$

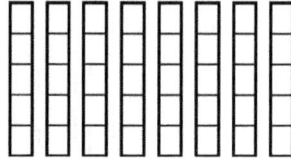

3) $\frac{7}{8} \times 8 =$

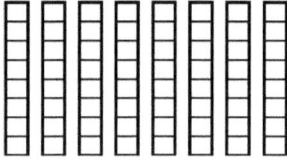

4) $\frac{6}{10} \times 5 =$

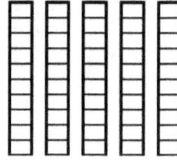

5) $\frac{2}{3} \times 3 =$

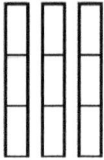

6) $\frac{6}{8} \times 5 =$

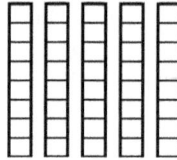

7) $\frac{5}{8} \times 4 =$

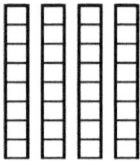

8) $\frac{1}{3} \times 8 =$

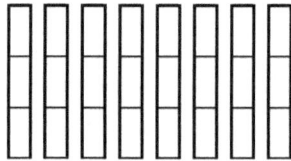

9) $\frac{3}{8} \times 8 =$

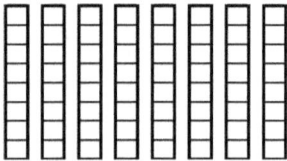

10) $\frac{6}{8} \times 7 =$

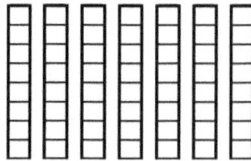

1. _____

2. _____

3. _____

4. _____

5. _____

6. _____

7. _____

8. _____

9. _____

10. _____

1) $\frac{1}{10} \times 9 =$

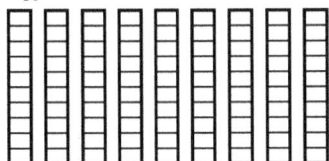

2) $\frac{3}{10} \times 6 =$

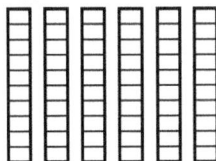

3) $\frac{3}{5} \times 4 =$

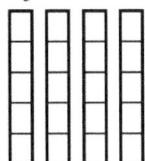

4) $\frac{4}{6} \times 8 =$

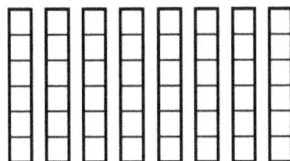

5) $\frac{3}{4} \times 9 =$

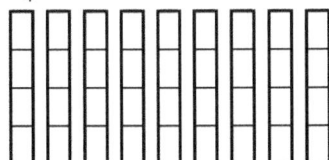

6) $\frac{2}{5} \times 3 =$

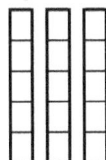

7) $\frac{1}{3} \times 7 =$

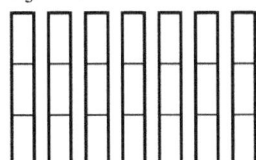

8) $\frac{3}{10} \times 3 =$

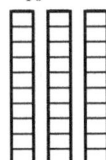

9) $\frac{3}{6} \times 8 =$

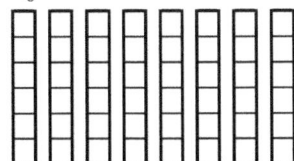

10) $\frac{1}{2} \times 5 =$

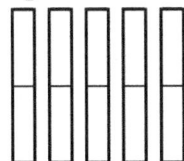

1. _____

2. _____

3. _____

4. _____

5. _____

6. _____

7. _____

8. _____

9. _____

10. _____

1) $\frac{4}{6} \times 9 =$

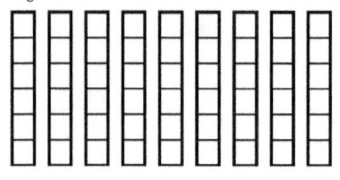

2) $\frac{2}{10} \times 2 =$

3) $\frac{4}{8} \times 4 =$

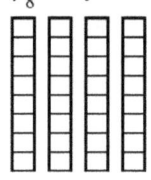

4) $\frac{4}{8} \times 4 =$

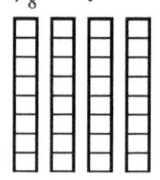

5) $\frac{1}{2} \times 7 =$

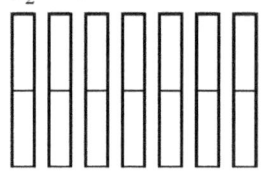

6) $\frac{1}{2} \times 2 =$

7) $\frac{2}{4} \times 6 =$

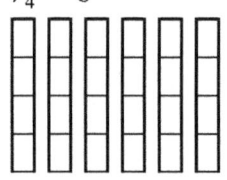

8) $\frac{2}{3} \times 8 =$

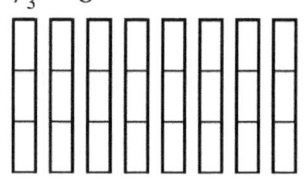

9) $\frac{2}{4} \times 8 =$

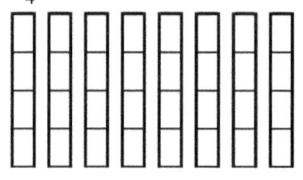

10) $\frac{4}{6} \times 6 =$

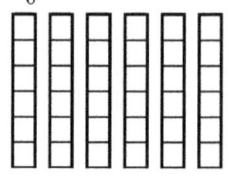

1. _____
2. _____
3. _____
4. _____
5. _____
6. _____
7. _____
8. _____
9. _____
10. _____

1) $\frac{1}{5} \times 3 =$

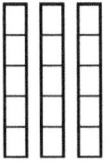

2) $\frac{2}{8} \times 9 =$

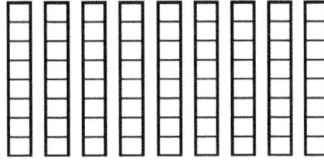

3) $\frac{3}{4} \times 4 =$

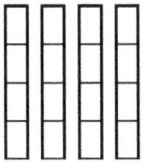

4) $\frac{2}{4} \times 3 =$

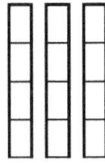

5) $\frac{2}{3} \times 3 =$

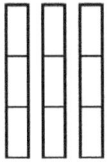

6) $\frac{1}{2} \times 3 =$

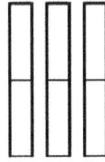

7) $\frac{1}{6} \times 7 =$

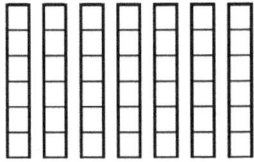

8) $\frac{3}{4} \times 6 =$

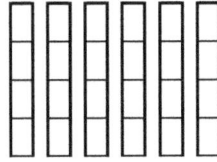

9) $\frac{3}{8} \times 3 =$

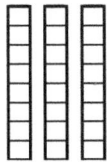

10) $\frac{5}{8} \times 5 =$

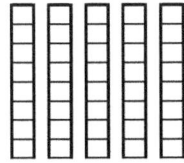

1. _____
2. _____
3. _____
4. _____
5. _____
6. _____
7. _____
8. _____
9. _____
10. _____

Determine which fraction goes in the middle to make the comparison true. Choose the answer below.

1) $\frac{1}{6}$ $\frac{2}{3}$
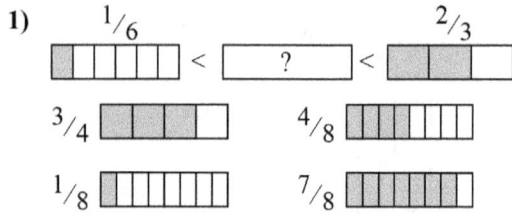
$\frac{3}{4}$ $\frac{4}{8}$
$\frac{1}{8}$ $\frac{7}{8}$

2) $\frac{1}{6}$ $\frac{2}{4}$
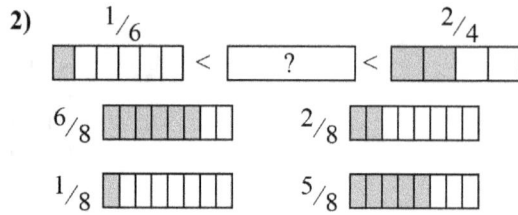
$\frac{6}{8}$ $\frac{2}{8}$
$\frac{1}{8}$ $\frac{5}{8}$

Ex.
4/8

1. _____
2. _____
3. _____
4. _____
5. _____
6. _____
7. _____
8. _____
9. _____
10. _____

3) $\frac{1}{3}$ $\frac{5}{8}$
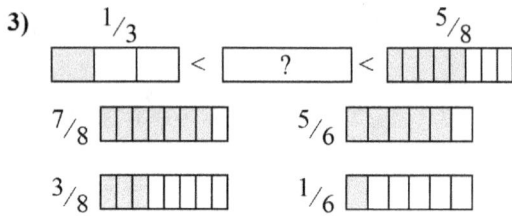
$\frac{7}{8}$ $\frac{5}{6}$
$\frac{3}{8}$ $\frac{1}{6}$

4) $\frac{1}{4}$ $\frac{3}{4}$
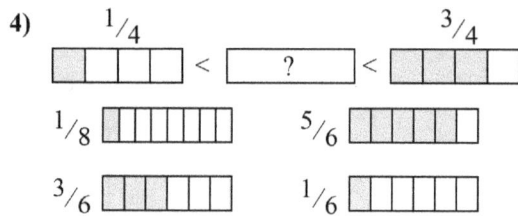
$\frac{1}{8}$ $\frac{5}{6}$
$\frac{3}{6}$ $\frac{1}{6}$

5) $\frac{2}{8}$ $\frac{3}{8}$
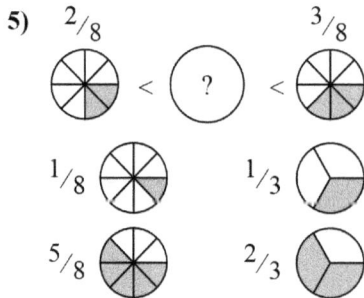
$\frac{1}{8}$ $\frac{1}{3}$
$\frac{5}{8}$ $\frac{2}{3}$

6) $\frac{4}{6}$ $\frac{5}{6}$
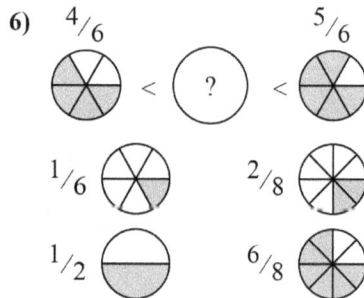
$\frac{1}{6}$ $\frac{2}{8}$
$\frac{1}{2}$ $\frac{6}{8}$

7) $\frac{1}{4}$ $\frac{4}{8}$
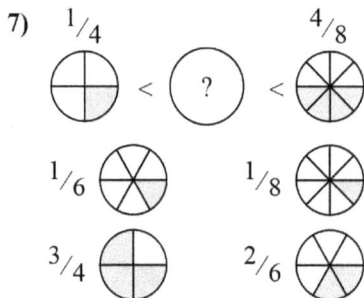
$\frac{1}{6}$ $\frac{1}{8}$
$\frac{3}{4}$ $\frac{2}{6}$

8) $\frac{1}{6}$ $\frac{3}{8}$
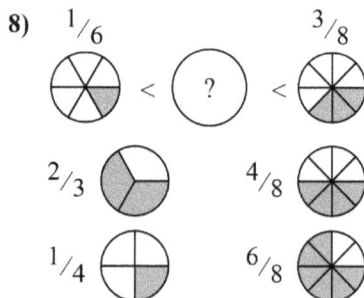
$\frac{2}{3}$ $\frac{4}{8}$
$\frac{1}{4}$ $\frac{6}{8}$

9) $\frac{2}{6}$ $\frac{3}{6}$
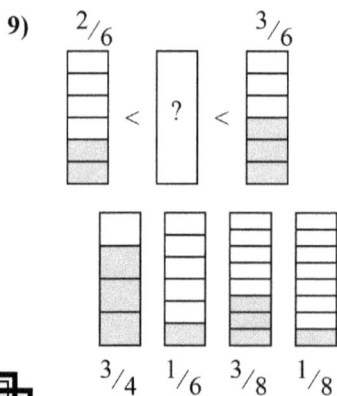
$\frac{3}{4}$ $\frac{1}{6}$ $\frac{3}{8}$ $\frac{1}{8}$

10) $\frac{1}{4}$ $\frac{3}{8}$
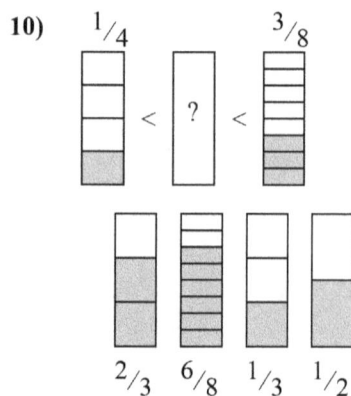
$\frac{2}{3}$ $\frac{6}{8}$ $\frac{1}{3}$ $\frac{1}{2}$

42

1) $\frac{1}{8}$ < ? < $\frac{2}{8}$

$\frac{2}{3}$ $\frac{5}{6}$

$\frac{6}{8}$ $\frac{1}{6}$

2) $\frac{4}{6}$ < ? < $\frac{5}{6}$

$\frac{1}{3}$ $\frac{1}{6}$

$\frac{2}{8}$ $\frac{6}{8}$

3) $\frac{1}{3}$ < ? < $\frac{5}{8}$

$\frac{2}{3}$ $\frac{2}{8}$

$\frac{3}{4}$ $\frac{3}{6}$

4) $\frac{4}{8}$ < ? < $\frac{2}{3}$

$\frac{1}{6}$ $\frac{5}{8}$

$\frac{6}{8}$ $\frac{1}{8}$

5) $\frac{3}{6}$ < ? < $\frac{2}{3}$

$\frac{5}{6}$ $\frac{3}{8}$

$\frac{2}{6}$ $\frac{5}{8}$

6) $\frac{2}{8}$ < ? < $\frac{3}{8}$

$\frac{1}{3}$ $\frac{3}{4}$

$\frac{1}{2}$ $\frac{1}{6}$

7) $\frac{5}{8}$ < ? < $\frac{6}{8}$

$\frac{2}{8}$ $\frac{2}{3}$

$\frac{7}{8}$ $\frac{5}{6}$

8) $\frac{4}{8}$ < ? < $\frac{4}{6}$

$\frac{3}{8}$ $\frac{2}{6}$

$\frac{5}{6}$ $\frac{5}{8}$

9) $\frac{1}{3}$ < ? < $\frac{5}{8}$

$\frac{3}{6}$ $\frac{1}{8}$ $\frac{1}{4}$ $\frac{4}{6}$

10) $\frac{2}{6}$ < ? < $\frac{2}{4}$

$\frac{3}{8}$ $\frac{5}{8}$ $\frac{3}{4}$ $\frac{2}{3}$

1. _____

2. _____

3. _____

4. _____

5. _____

6. _____

7. _____

8. _____

9. _____

10. _____

1)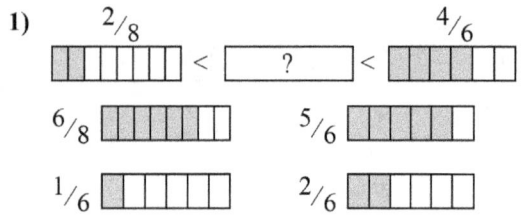

2)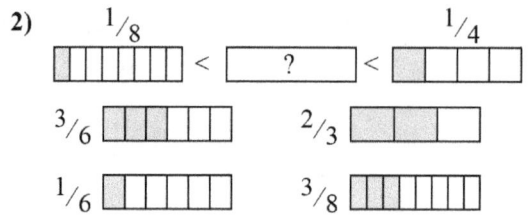

1. _____

2. _____

3)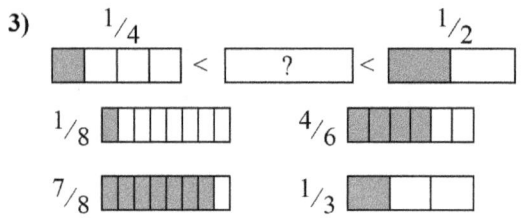

4)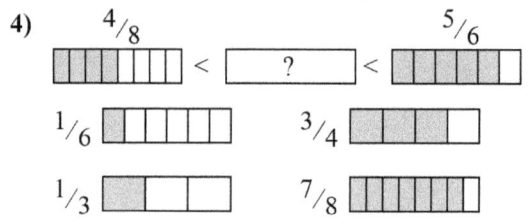

3. _____

4. _____

5)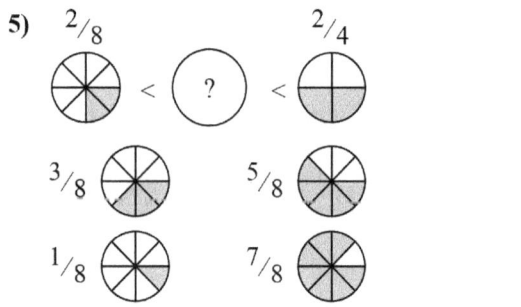

6)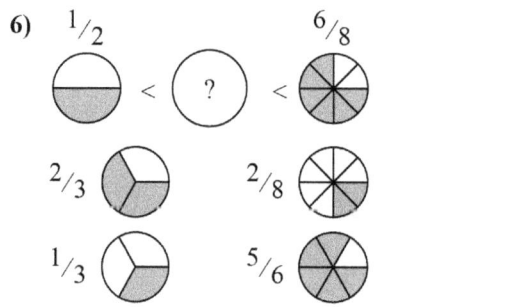

5. _____

6. _____

7. _____

7)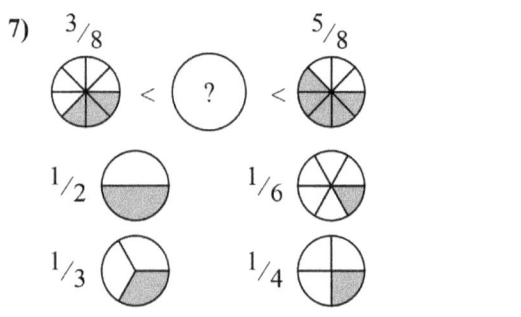

8)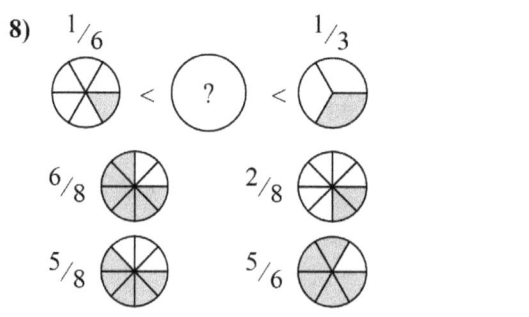

8. _____

9. _____

10. _____

9)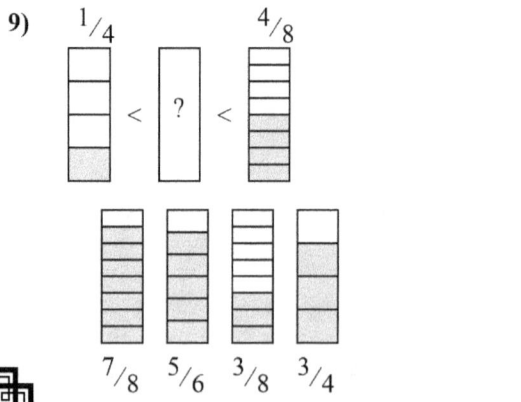

10)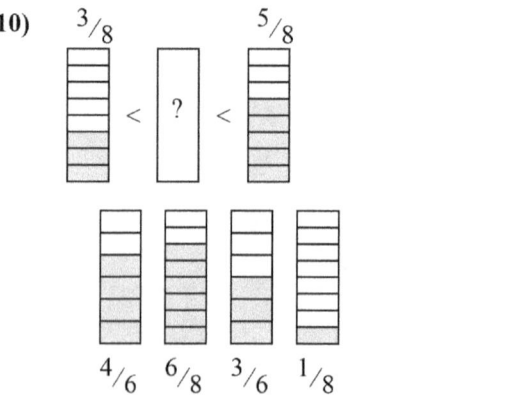

1)
$^2/_4$ < ? < $^3/_4$
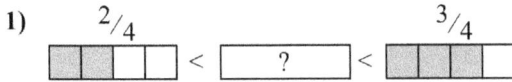
$^1/_6$ $^7/_8$

$^2/_6$ $^2/_3$
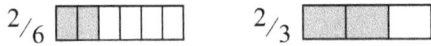

2)
$^3/_8$ < ? < $^5/_8$
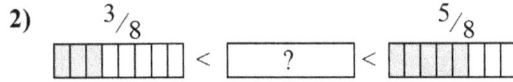
$^1/_6$ $^4/_6$

$^1/_2$ $^1/_8$

1. _____
2. _____
3. _____

3)
$^1/_8$ < ? < $^4/_8$
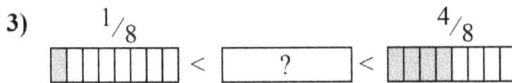
$^7/_8$ $^2/_3$

$^3/_4$ $^1/_3$
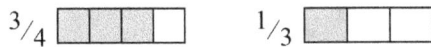

4)
$^1/_8$ < ? < $^4/_8$
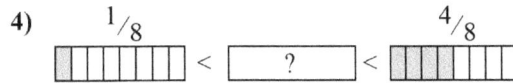
$^7/_8$ $^2/_6$

$^5/_8$ $^2/_3$

4. _____
5. _____
6. _____

5)
$^5/_8$ < ? < $^5/_6$
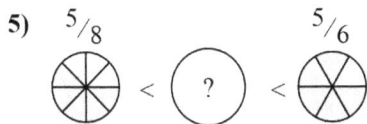
$^2/_8$ $^4/_8$

$^1/_3$ $^2/_3$

6)
$^3/_8$ < ? < $^5/_8$
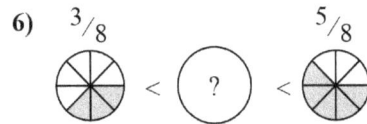
$^3/_4$ $^1/_3$

$^3/_6$ $^1/_8$

7. _____
8. _____
9. _____
10. _____

7)
$^1/_8$ < ? < $^1/_3$
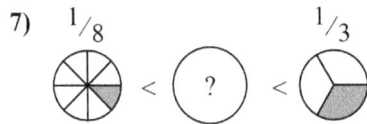
$^5/_6$ $^4/_8$

$^1/_4$ $^6/_8$

8)
$^1/_4$ < ? < $^2/_3$
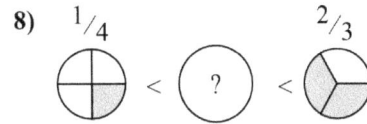
$^1/_8$ $^6/_8$

$^5/_6$ $^1/_2$

9)
$^1/_2$ < ? < $^7/_8$
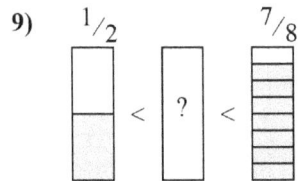
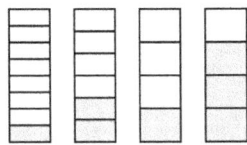
$^1/_8$ $^2/_6$ $^1/_4$ $^3/_4$

10)
$^1/_6$ < ? < $^1/_3$
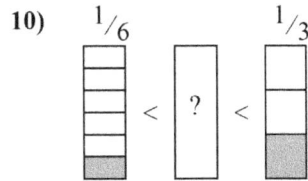
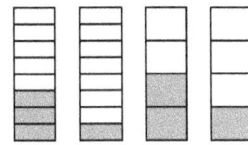
$^3/_8$ $^1/_8$ $^2/_4$ $^1/_4$

1) $\frac{1}{6}$ $\frac{2}{6}$

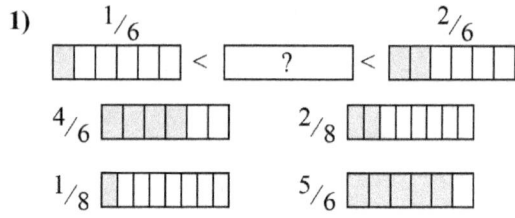

$\frac{4}{6}$ $\frac{2}{8}$

$\frac{1}{8}$ $\frac{5}{6}$

2) $\frac{2}{3}$ $\frac{5}{6}$

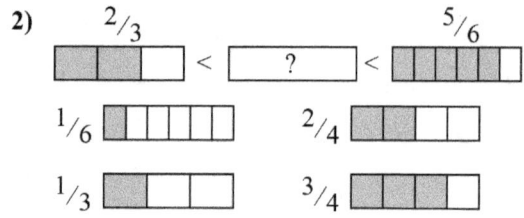

$\frac{1}{6}$ $\frac{2}{4}$

$\frac{1}{3}$ $\frac{3}{4}$

3) $\frac{1}{2}$ $\frac{5}{6}$

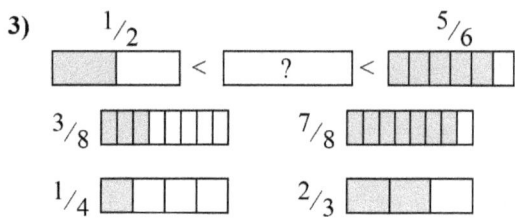

$\frac{3}{8}$ $\frac{7}{8}$

$\frac{1}{4}$ $\frac{2}{3}$

4) $\frac{1}{4}$ $\frac{3}{8}$

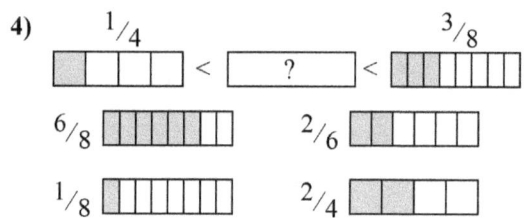

$\frac{6}{8}$ $\frac{2}{6}$

$\frac{1}{8}$ $\frac{2}{4}$

5) $\frac{1}{3}$ $\frac{4}{6}$

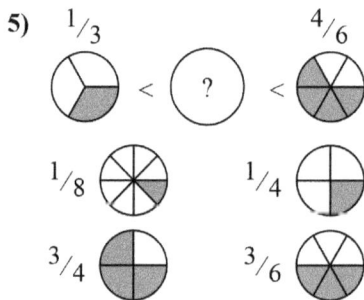

$\frac{1}{8}$ $\frac{1}{4}$

$\frac{3}{4}$ $\frac{3}{6}$

6) $\frac{2}{6}$ $\frac{2}{3}$

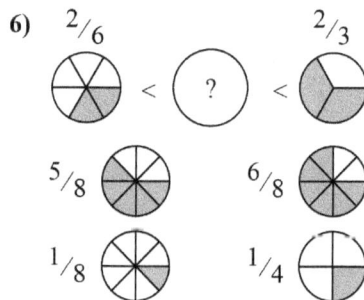

$\frac{5}{8}$ $\frac{6}{8}$

$\frac{1}{8}$ $\frac{1}{4}$

7) $\frac{1}{8}$ $\frac{1}{3}$

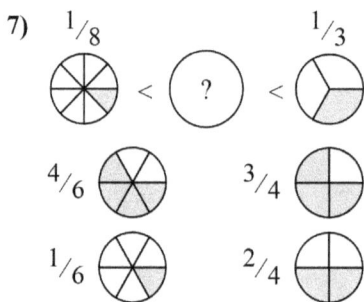

$\frac{4}{6}$ $\frac{3}{4}$

$\frac{1}{6}$ $\frac{2}{4}$

8) $\frac{1}{2}$ $\frac{3}{4}$

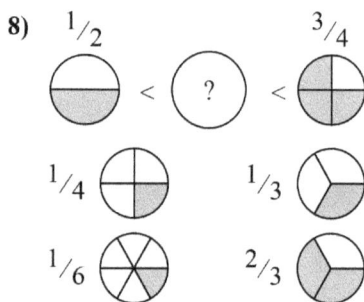

$\frac{1}{4}$ $\frac{1}{3}$

$\frac{1}{6}$ $\frac{2}{3}$

9) $\frac{1}{8}$ $\frac{3}{8}$

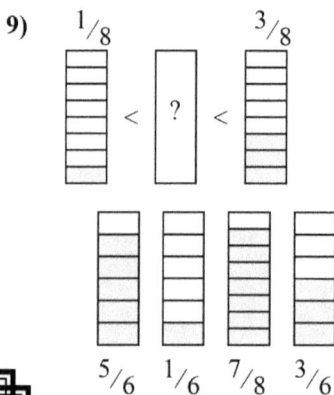

$\frac{5}{6}$ $\frac{1}{6}$ $\frac{7}{8}$ $\frac{3}{6}$

10) $\frac{4}{8}$ $\frac{5}{6}$

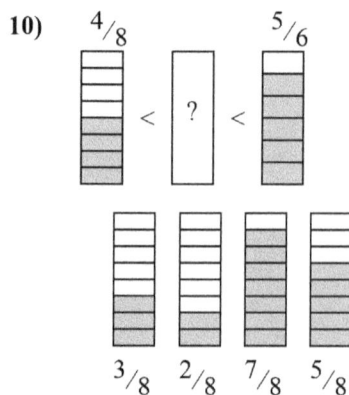

$\frac{3}{8}$ $\frac{2}{8}$ $\frac{7}{8}$ $\frac{5}{8}$

1. _____

2. _____

3. _____

4. _____

5. _____

6. _____

7. _____

8. _____

9. _____

10. _____

46

1) $^3/_8$ < ? < $^2/_3$

$^2/_4$ $^3/_4$

$^5/_6$ $^1/_8$

2) $^2/_6$ < ? < $^4/_6$

$^3/_4$ $^7/_8$

$^5/_8$ $^1/_8$

3) $^1/_6$ < ? < $^1/_3$

$^2/_3$ $^2/_8$

$^1/_8$ $^1/_2$

4) $^4/_6$ < ? < $^7/_8$

$^5/_8$ $^1/_2$

$^3/_4$ $^2/_8$

5) $^2/_6$ < ? < $^5/_8$

$^6/_8$ $^2/_8$

$^3/_8$ $^4/_6$

6) $^3/_6$ < ? < $^6/_8$

$^7/_8$ $^1/_8$

$^2/_3$ $^1/_3$

7) $^3/_8$ < ? < $^5/_8$

$^5/_6$ $^2/_3$

$^1/_8$ $^4/_8$

8) $^1/_3$ < ? < $^2/_3$

$^4/_8$ $^7/_8$

$^1/_6$ $^6/_8$

9) $^1/_4$ < ? < $^4/_8$

$^7/_8$ $^2/_6$ $^3/_4$ $^4/_6$

10) $^1/_8$ < ? < $^2/_6$

$^1/_6$ $^1/_2$ $^3/_8$ $^5/_8$

1. _____

2. _____

3. _____

4. _____

5. _____

6. _____

7. _____

8. _____

9. _____

10. _____

1)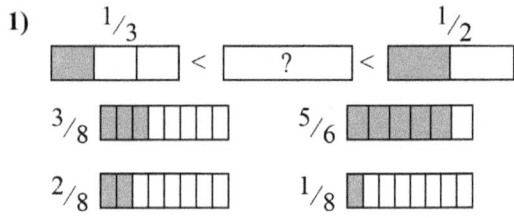

2)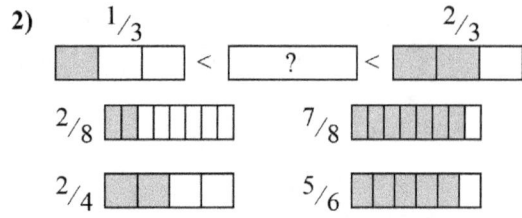

3)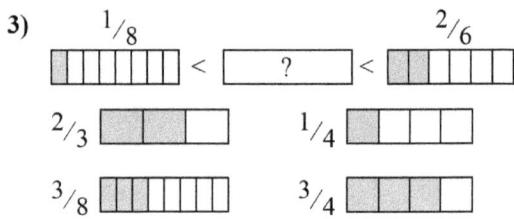

4)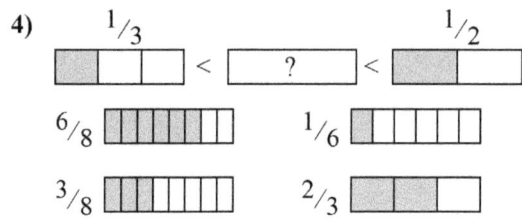

5)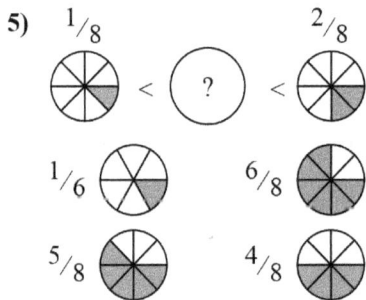

6)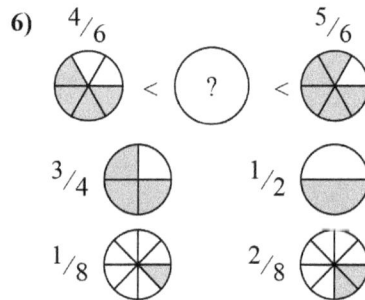

7)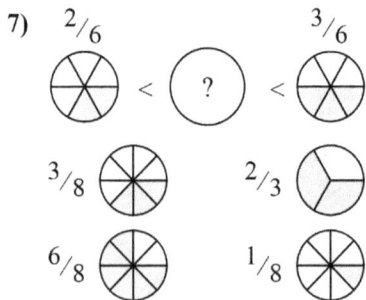

8)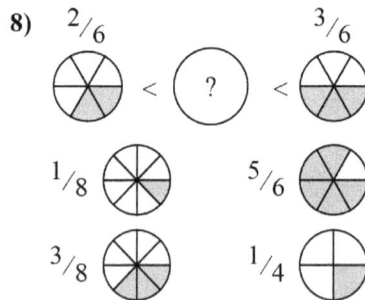

9)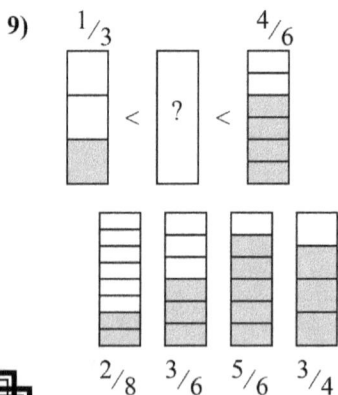

10)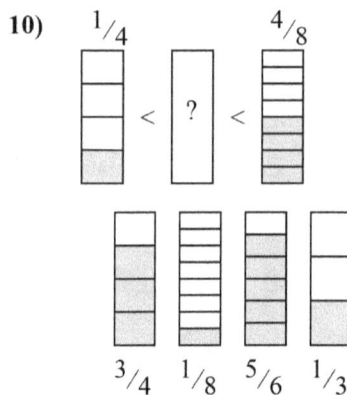

1. _____
2. _____
3. _____
4. _____
5. _____
6. _____
7. _____
8. _____
9. _____
10. _____

1)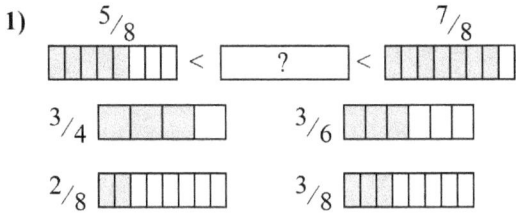

2)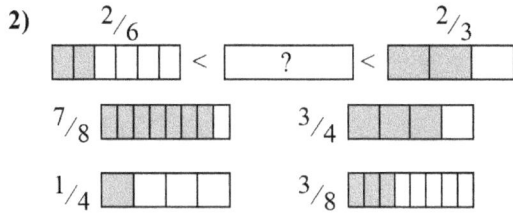

1. _____

2. _____

3)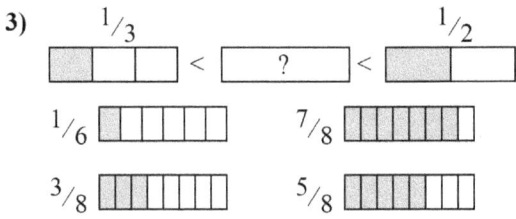

4)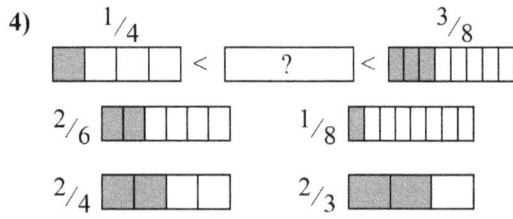

3. _____

4. _____

5)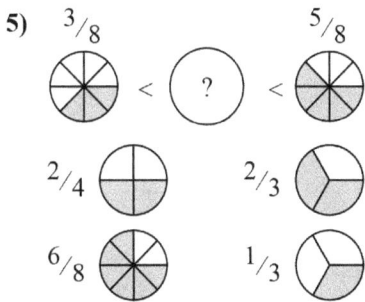

6)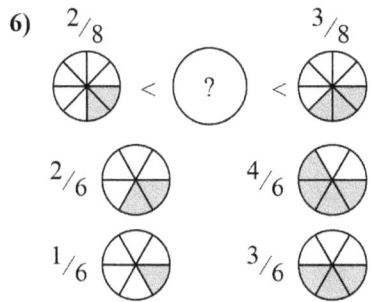

5. _____

6. _____

7. _____

7)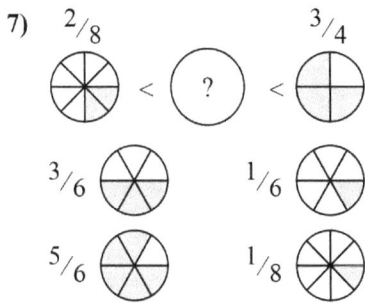

8)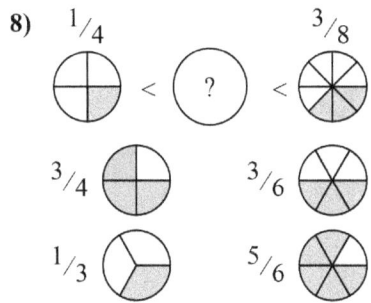

8. _____

9. _____

10. _____

9)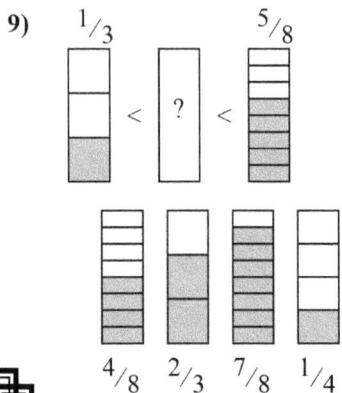

10)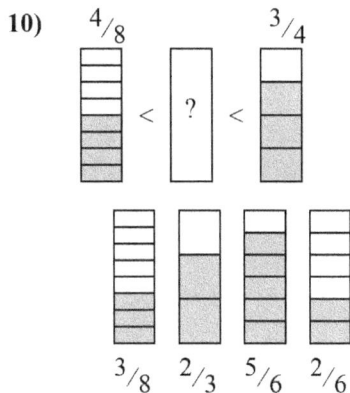

1) $\frac{4}{8}$ [ ] < [?] < $\frac{2}{3}$ [ ]

$\frac{1}{3}$ [ ] $\frac{3}{8}$ [ ]

$\frac{5}{8}$ [ ] $\frac{1}{6}$ [ ]

2) $\frac{2}{6}$ [ ] < [?] < $\frac{4}{6}$ [ ]

$\frac{1}{2}$ [ ] $\frac{1}{6}$ [ ]

$\frac{3}{4}$ [ ] $\frac{7}{8}$ [ ]

3) $\frac{4}{6}$ [ ] < [?] < $\frac{5}{6}$ [ ]

$\frac{3}{6}$ [ ] $\frac{1}{3}$ [ ]

$\frac{6}{8}$ [ ] $\frac{1}{8}$ [ ]

4) $\frac{4}{6}$ [ ] < [?] < $\frac{7}{8}$ [ ]

$\frac{1}{3}$ [ ] $\frac{2}{4}$ [ ]

$\frac{5}{8}$ [ ] $\frac{6}{8}$ [ ]

5) $\frac{1}{4}$ ◯ < ◯? < $\frac{1}{2}$ ◯

$\frac{5}{8}$ ◯ $\frac{7}{8}$ ◯

$\frac{1}{3}$ ◯ $\frac{5}{6}$ ◯

6) $\frac{1}{8}$ ◯ < ◯? < $\frac{4}{6}$ ◯

$\frac{7}{8}$ ◯ $\frac{1}{6}$ ◯

$\frac{6}{8}$ ◯ $\frac{5}{6}$ ◯

7) $\frac{5}{8}$ ◯ < ◯? < $\frac{5}{6}$ ◯

$\frac{1}{8}$ ◯ $\frac{1}{3}$ ◯

$\frac{3}{4}$ ◯ $\frac{1}{4}$ ◯

8) $\frac{3}{8}$ ◯ < ◯? < $\frac{5}{8}$ ◯

$\frac{1}{2}$ ◯ $\frac{7}{8}$ ◯

$\frac{2}{8}$ ◯ $\frac{5}{6}$ ◯

9) $\frac{5}{8}$ [ ] < [?] < $\frac{6}{8}$ [ ]

$\frac{4}{8}$ $\frac{1}{4}$ $\frac{2}{6}$ $\frac{2}{3}$

10) $\frac{4}{8}$ [ ] < [?] < $\frac{2}{3}$ [ ]

$\frac{5}{8}$ $\frac{1}{8}$ $\frac{1}{6}$ $\frac{2}{6}$

1. _____
2. _____
3. _____
4. _____
5. _____
6. _____
7. _____
8. _____
9. _____
10. _____

1) 4/8 < ? < 4/6

1/3   2/8

7/8   5/8

2) 2/8 < ? < 3/6

5/6   1/6

3/8   1/8

3) 1/2 < ? < 2/3

5/8   6/8

1/3   1/8

4) 1/4 < ? < 2/3

5/6   3/4

1/6   2/4

5) 2/4 < ? < 5/6

2/8   3/8

3/4   2/6

6) 3/6 < ? < 3/4

3/8   1/3

1/4   2/3

7) 2/6 < ? < 4/6

6/8   1/6

3/8   2/8

8) 4/8 < ? < 5/6

7/8   1/8

2/6   2/3

9) 3/6 < ? < 7/8

1/6   4/6   1/4   2/6

10) 1/8 < ? < 3/8

1/4   7/8   2/4   6/8

1. _____
2. _____
3. _____
4. _____
5. _____
6. _____
7. _____
8. _____
9. _____
10. _____

Determine which letter best represents an equivalent fraction. Choose the answer below.

1)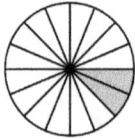
$\dfrac{2}{16}$

2)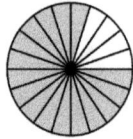
$\dfrac{16}{20}$

3)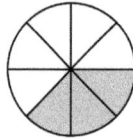
$\dfrac{3}{8}$

4)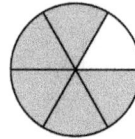
$\dfrac{5}{6}$

5)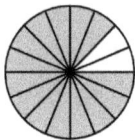
$\dfrac{14}{16}$

6)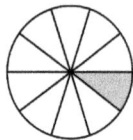
$\dfrac{1}{10}$

7)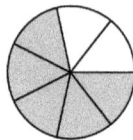
$\dfrac{5}{7}$

8)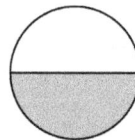
$\dfrac{1}{2}$

9)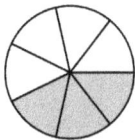
$\dfrac{3}{7}$

10)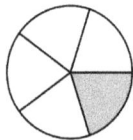
$\dfrac{1}{5}$

11)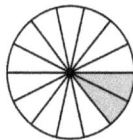
$\dfrac{2}{14}$

12)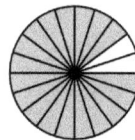
$\dfrac{18}{20}$

Ex.
1. _I_
2. _____
3. _____
4. _____
5. _____
6. _____
7. _____
8. _____
9. _____
10. _____
11. _____
12. _____

A)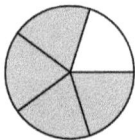
$\dfrac{4}{5}$

B)
$\dfrac{6}{16}$

C)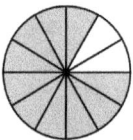
$\dfrac{10}{12}$

D)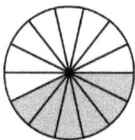
$\dfrac{6}{14}$

E)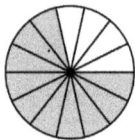
$\dfrac{10}{14}$

F)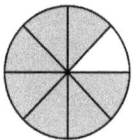
$\dfrac{7}{8}$

G)
$\dfrac{5}{10}$

H)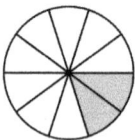
$\dfrac{2}{10}$

I)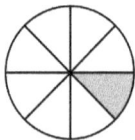
$\dfrac{1}{8}$

J)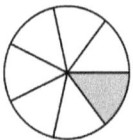
$\dfrac{1}{7}$

K)
$\dfrac{2}{20}$

L)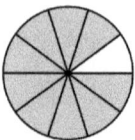
$\dfrac{9}{10}$

1)

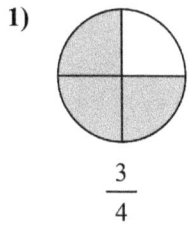

$$\frac{3}{4}$$

2)

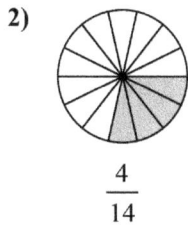

$$\frac{4}{14}$$

3)

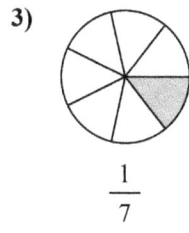

$$\frac{1}{7}$$

4)

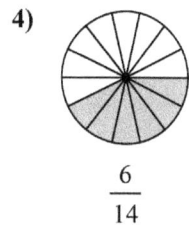

$$\frac{6}{14}$$

5)

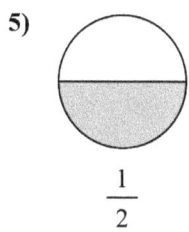

$$\frac{1}{2}$$

6)

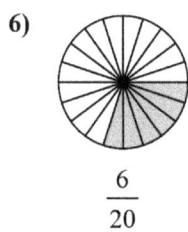

$$\frac{6}{20}$$

7)

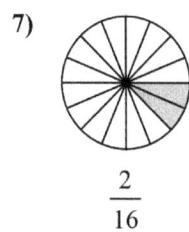

$$\frac{2}{16}$$

8)

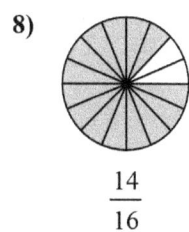

$$\frac{14}{16}$$

9)

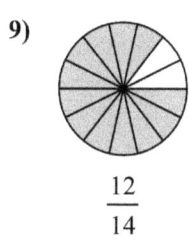

$$\frac{12}{14}$$

10)

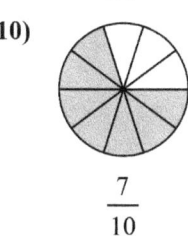

$$\frac{7}{10}$$

11)

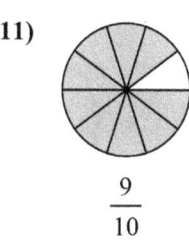

$$\frac{9}{10}$$

12)

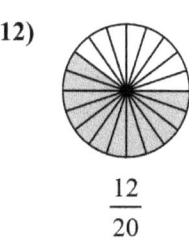

$$\frac{12}{20}$$

1. _____

2. _____

3. _____

4. _____

5. _____

6. _____

7. _____

8. _____

9. _____

10. _____

11. _____

12. _____

A)

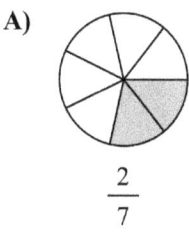

$$\frac{2}{7}$$

B)

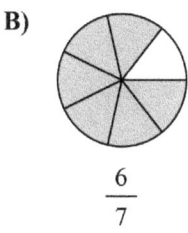

$$\frac{6}{7}$$

C)

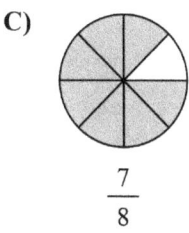

$$\frac{7}{8}$$

D)

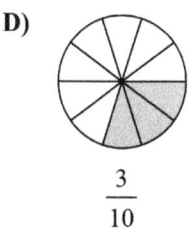

$$\frac{3}{10}$$

E)

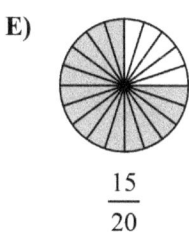

$$\frac{15}{20}$$

F)

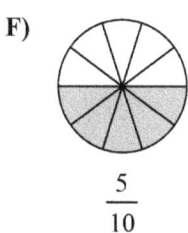

$$\frac{5}{10}$$

G)

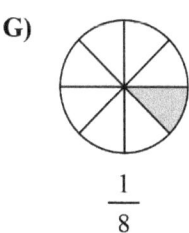

$$\frac{1}{8}$$

H)

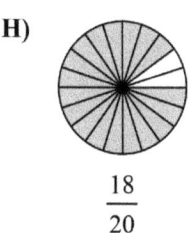

$$\frac{18}{20}$$

I)

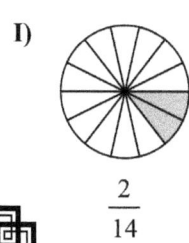

$$\frac{2}{14}$$

J)

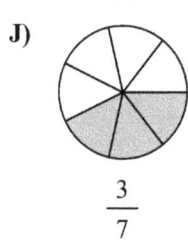

$$\frac{3}{7}$$

K)

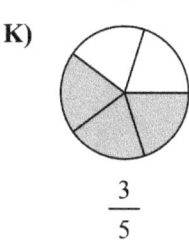

$$\frac{3}{5}$$

L)

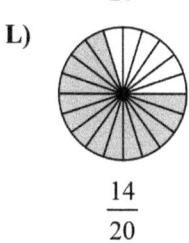

$$\frac{14}{20}$$

1)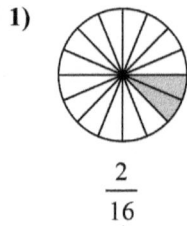
$\dfrac{2}{16}$

2)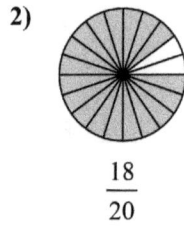
$\dfrac{18}{20}$

3)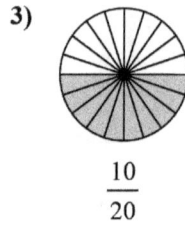
$\dfrac{10}{20}$

4)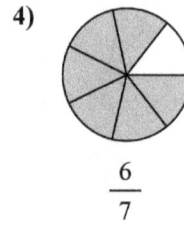
$\dfrac{6}{7}$

5)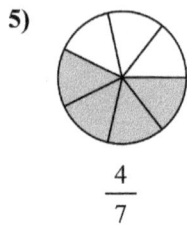
$\dfrac{4}{7}$

6)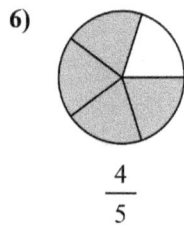
$\dfrac{4}{5}$

7)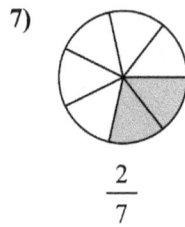
$\dfrac{2}{7}$

8)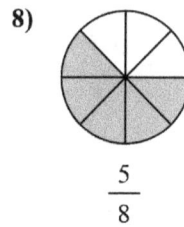
$\dfrac{5}{8}$

9)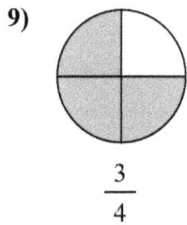
$\dfrac{3}{4}$

10)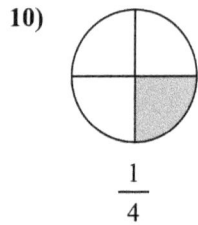
$\dfrac{1}{4}$

11)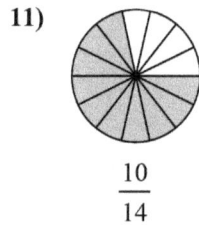
$\dfrac{10}{14}$

12)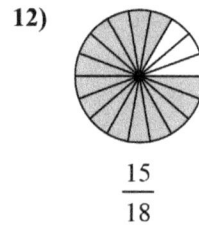
$\dfrac{15}{18}$

A)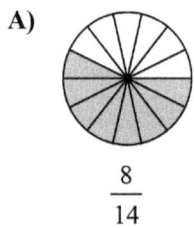
$\dfrac{8}{14}$

B)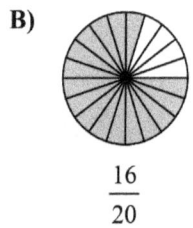
$\dfrac{16}{20}$

C)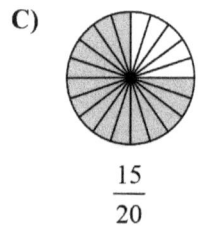
$\dfrac{15}{20}$

D)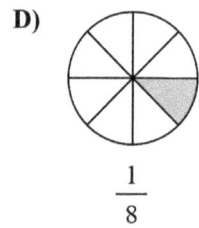
$\dfrac{1}{8}$

E)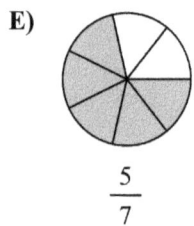
$\dfrac{5}{7}$

F)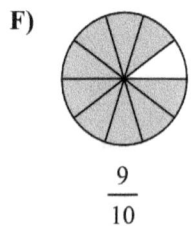
$\dfrac{9}{10}$

G)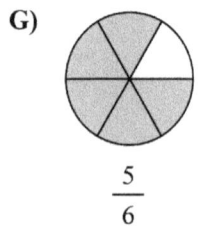
$\dfrac{5}{6}$

H)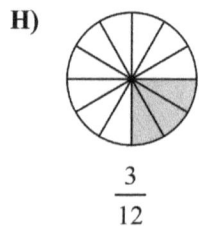
$\dfrac{3}{12}$

I)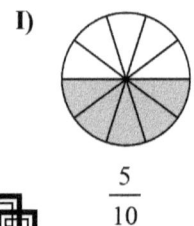
$\dfrac{5}{10}$

J)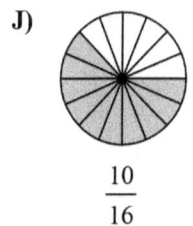
$\dfrac{10}{16}$

K)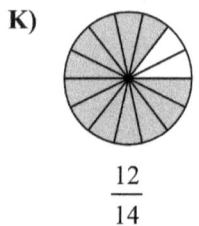
$\dfrac{12}{14}$

L)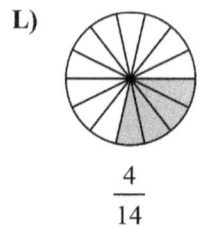
$\dfrac{4}{14}$

1. _____
2. _____
3. _____
4. _____
5. _____
6. _____
7. _____
8. _____
9. _____
10. _____
11. _____
12. _____

1)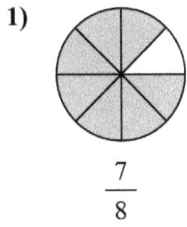

$\dfrac{7}{8}$

2)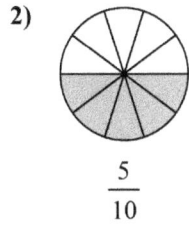

$\dfrac{5}{10}$

3)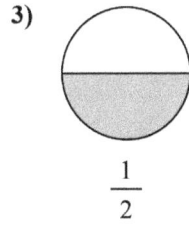

$\dfrac{1}{2}$

4)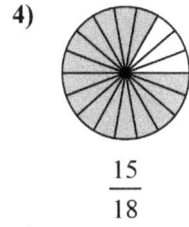

$\dfrac{15}{18}$

5)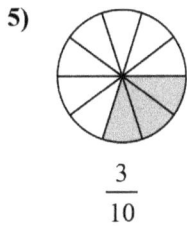

$\dfrac{3}{10}$

6)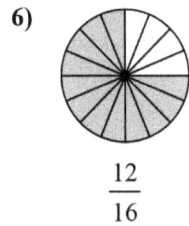

$\dfrac{12}{16}$

7)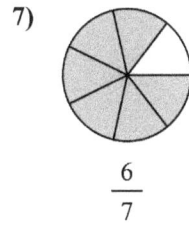

$\dfrac{6}{7}$

8)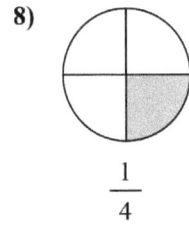

$\dfrac{1}{4}$

9)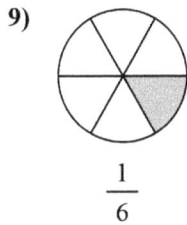

$\dfrac{1}{6}$

10)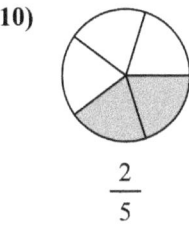

$\dfrac{2}{5}$

11)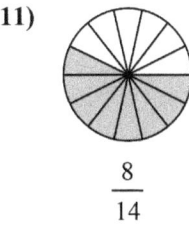

$\dfrac{8}{14}$

12)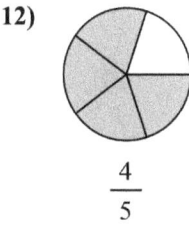

$\dfrac{4}{5}$

1. _____

2. _____

3. _____

4. _____

5. _____

6. _____

7. _____

8. _____

9. _____

10. _____

11. _____

12. _____

A)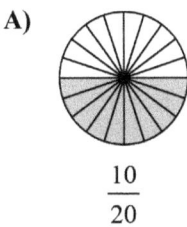

$\dfrac{10}{20}$

B)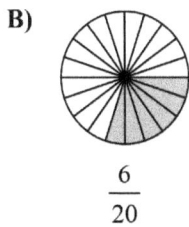

$\dfrac{6}{20}$

C)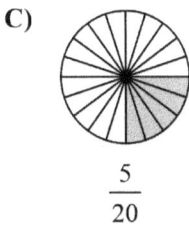

$\dfrac{5}{20}$

D)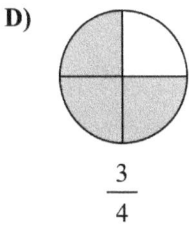

$\dfrac{3}{4}$

E)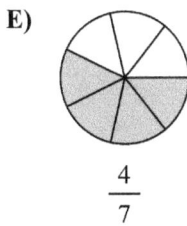

$\dfrac{4}{7}$

F)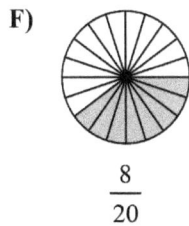

$\dfrac{8}{20}$

G)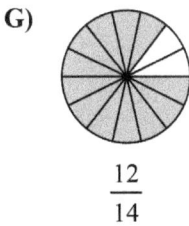

$\dfrac{12}{14}$

H)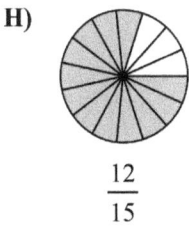

$\dfrac{12}{15}$

I)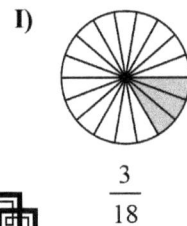

$\dfrac{3}{18}$

J)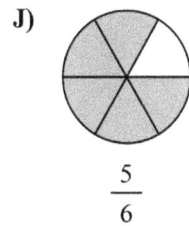

$\dfrac{5}{6}$

K)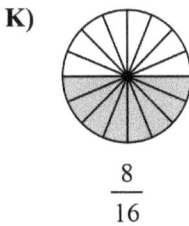

$\dfrac{8}{16}$

L)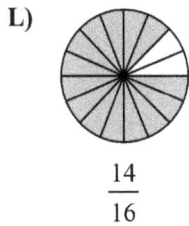

$\dfrac{14}{16}$

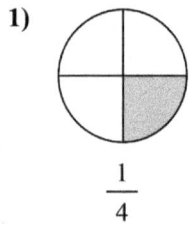

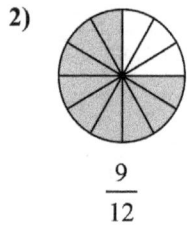

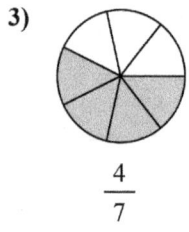

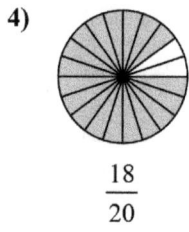

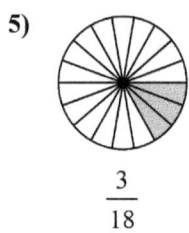

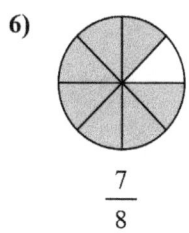

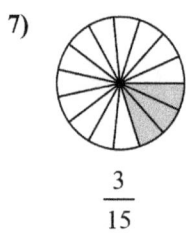

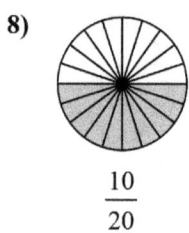

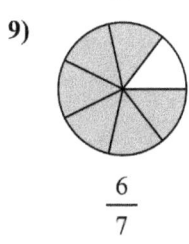

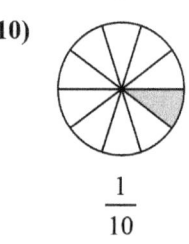

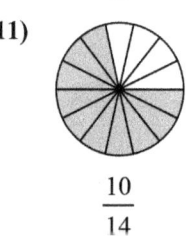

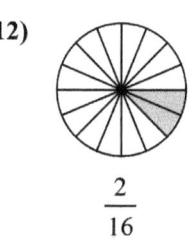

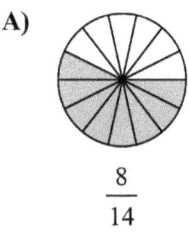

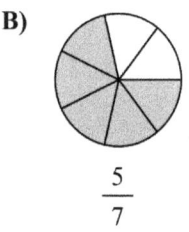

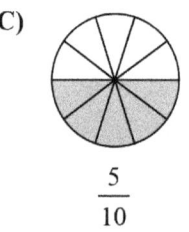

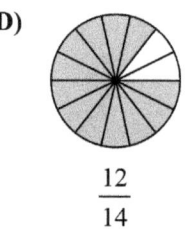

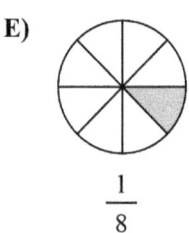

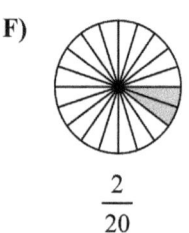

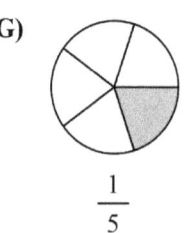

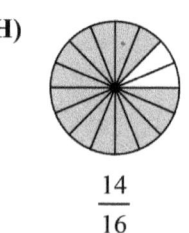

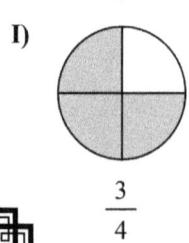

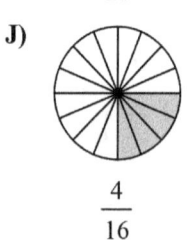

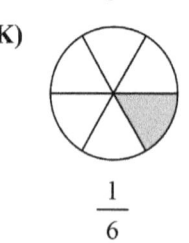

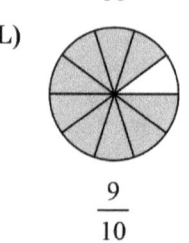

1)

$\dfrac{1}{4}$

2)

$\dfrac{9}{12}$

3)

$\dfrac{4}{7}$

4)

$\dfrac{18}{20}$

5)

$\dfrac{3}{18}$

6)

$\dfrac{7}{8}$

7)

$\dfrac{3}{15}$

8)

$\dfrac{10}{20}$

9)

$\dfrac{6}{7}$

10)

$\dfrac{1}{10}$

11)

$\dfrac{10}{14}$

12)

$\dfrac{2}{16}$

1. _____

2. _____

3. _____

4. _____

5. _____

6. _____

7. _____

8. _____

9. _____

10. _____

11. _____

12. _____

A)

$\dfrac{8}{14}$

B)

$\dfrac{5}{7}$

C)

$\dfrac{5}{10}$

D)

$\dfrac{12}{14}$

E)

$\dfrac{1}{8}$

F)

$\dfrac{2}{20}$

G)

$\dfrac{1}{5}$

H)

$\dfrac{14}{16}$

I)

$\dfrac{3}{4}$

J)

$\dfrac{4}{16}$

K)

$\dfrac{1}{6}$

L)

$\dfrac{9}{10}$

1)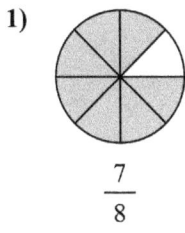

$\dfrac{7}{8}$

2)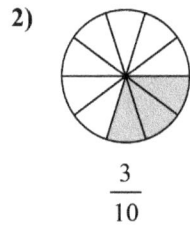

$\dfrac{3}{10}$

3)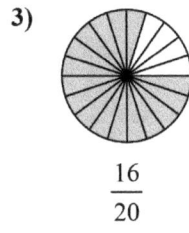

$\dfrac{16}{20}$

4)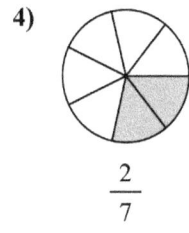

$\dfrac{2}{7}$

5)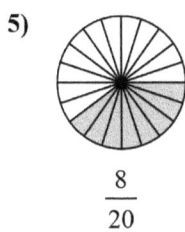

$\dfrac{8}{20}$

6)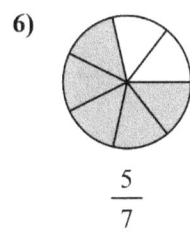

$\dfrac{5}{7}$

7)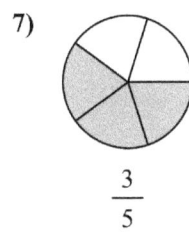

$\dfrac{3}{5}$

8)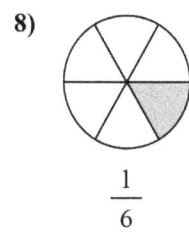

$\dfrac{1}{6}$

9)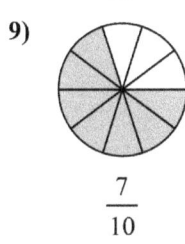

$\dfrac{7}{10}$

10)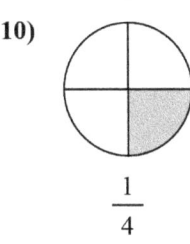

$\dfrac{1}{4}$

11)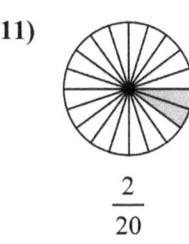

$\dfrac{2}{20}$

12)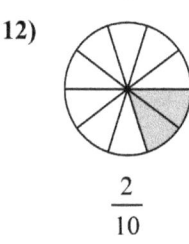

$\dfrac{2}{10}$

1. _____

2. _____

3. _____

4. _____

5. _____

6. _____

7. _____

8. _____

9. _____

10. _____

11. _____

12. _____

A)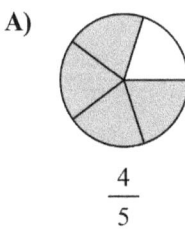

$\dfrac{4}{5}$

B)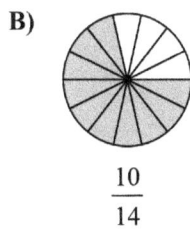

$\dfrac{10}{14}$

C)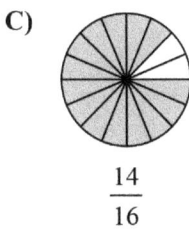

$\dfrac{14}{16}$

D)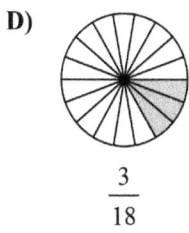

$\dfrac{3}{18}$

E)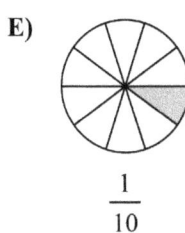

$\dfrac{1}{10}$

F)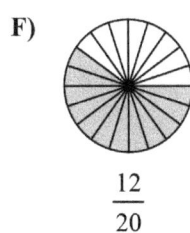

$\dfrac{12}{20}$

G)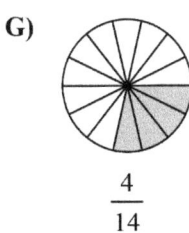

$\dfrac{4}{14}$

H)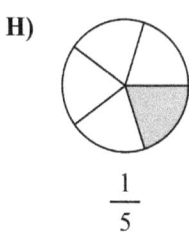

$\dfrac{1}{5}$

I)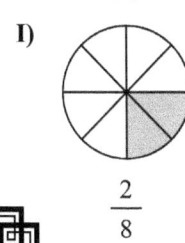

$\dfrac{2}{8}$

J)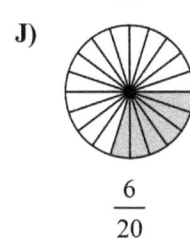

$\dfrac{6}{20}$

K)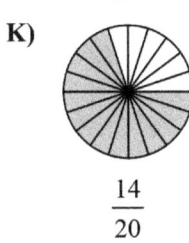

$\dfrac{14}{20}$

L)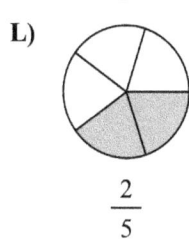

$\dfrac{2}{5}$

1)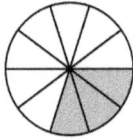

$\dfrac{3}{10}$

2)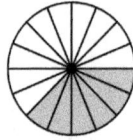

$\dfrac{6}{16}$

3)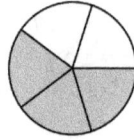

$\dfrac{3}{5}$

4)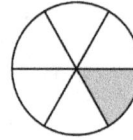

$\dfrac{1}{6}$

5)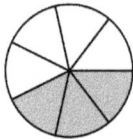

$\dfrac{3}{7}$

6)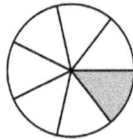

$\dfrac{1}{7}$

7)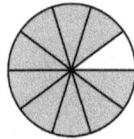

$\dfrac{9}{10}$

8)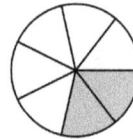

$\dfrac{2}{7}$

9)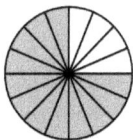

$\dfrac{12}{16}$

10)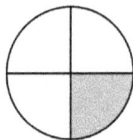

$\dfrac{1}{4}$

11)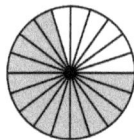

$\dfrac{14}{20}$

12)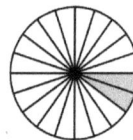

$\dfrac{2}{20}$

A)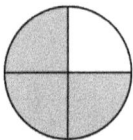

$\dfrac{3}{4}$

B)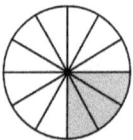

$\dfrac{3}{12}$

C)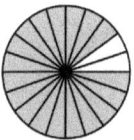

$\dfrac{18}{20}$

D)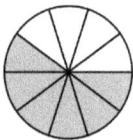

$\dfrac{6}{10}$

E)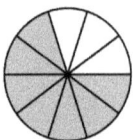

$\dfrac{7}{10}$

F)

$\dfrac{6}{20}$

G)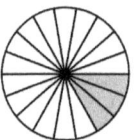

$\dfrac{3}{18}$

H)

$\dfrac{1}{10}$

I)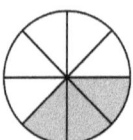

$\dfrac{3}{8}$

J)

$\dfrac{6}{14}$

K)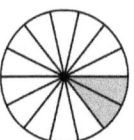

$\dfrac{2}{14}$

L)

$\dfrac{4}{14}$

1. _____

2. _____

3. _____

4. _____

5. _____

6. _____

7. _____

8. _____

9. _____

10. _____

11. _____

12. _____

58

1) $\frac{1}{7}$

2) $\frac{5}{6}$

3) $\frac{6}{16}$

4) $\frac{4}{14}$

5) $\frac{1}{6}$

6) $\frac{6}{14}$

7) $\frac{5}{7}$

8) $\frac{1}{2}$

9) $\frac{7}{10}$

10) $\frac{2}{16}$

11) $\frac{4}{7}$

12) $\frac{10}{16}$

A) $\frac{3}{8}$

B) $\frac{14}{20}$

C) $\frac{10}{12}$

D) $\frac{1}{8}$

E) $\frac{10}{14}$

F) $\frac{2}{14}$

G) $\frac{3}{6}$

H) $\frac{3}{7}$

I) $\frac{2}{12}$

J) $\frac{2}{7}$

K) $\frac{5}{8}$

L) $\frac{8}{14}$

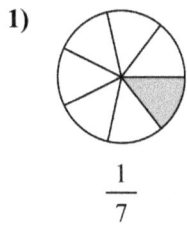

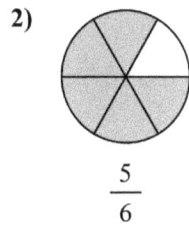

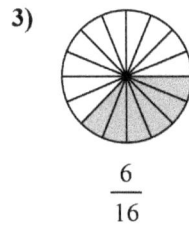

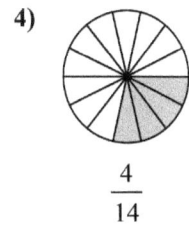

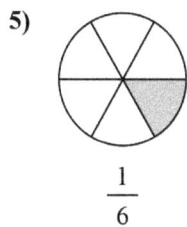

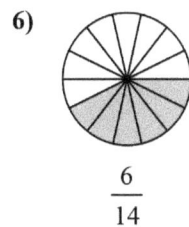

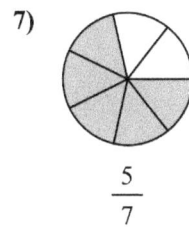

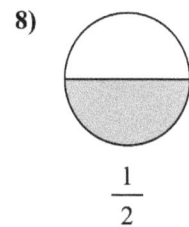

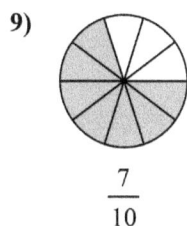

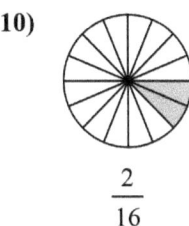

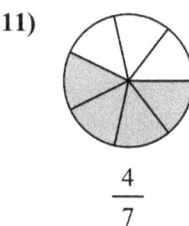

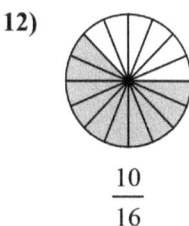

1. _____
2. _____
3. _____
4. _____
5. _____
6. _____
7. _____
8. _____
9. _____
10. _____
11. _____
12. _____

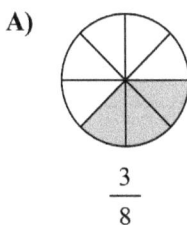

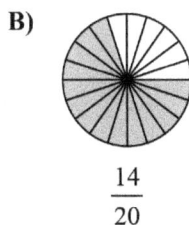

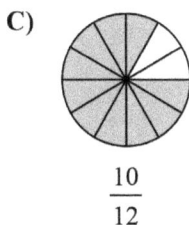

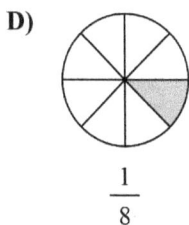

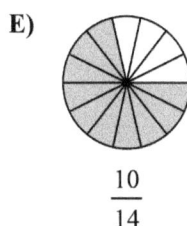

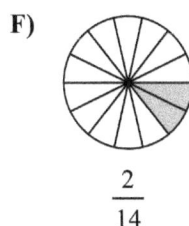

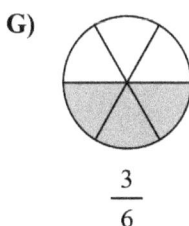

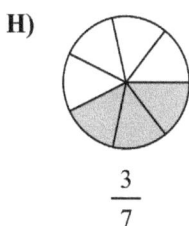

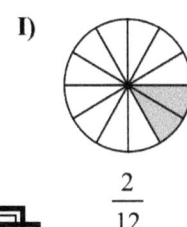

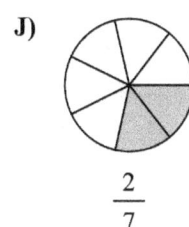

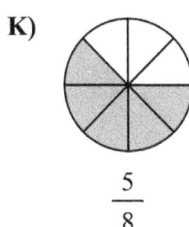

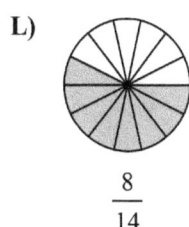

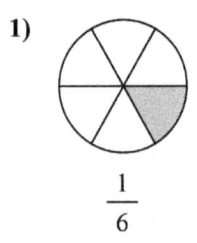

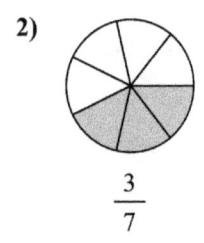

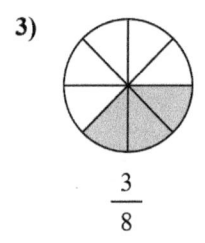

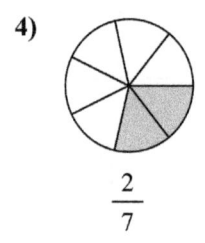

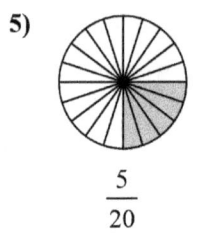

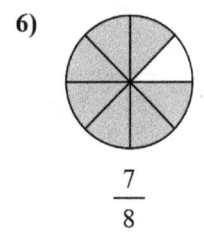

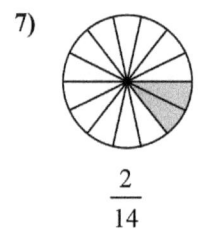

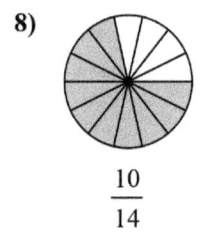

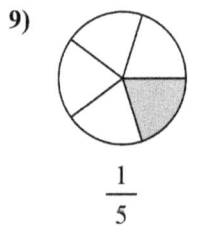

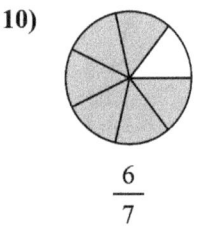

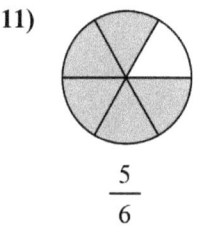

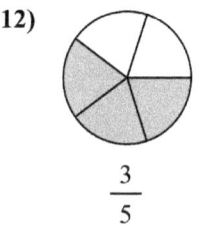

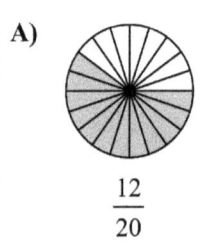

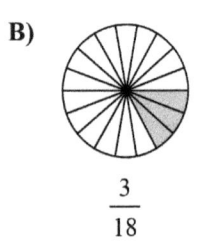

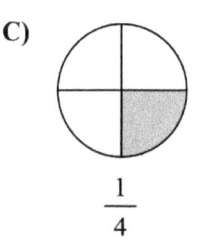

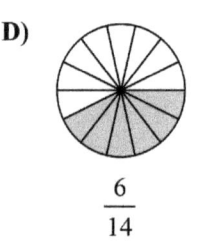

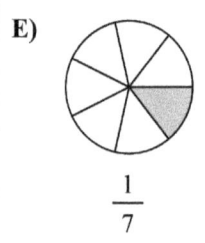

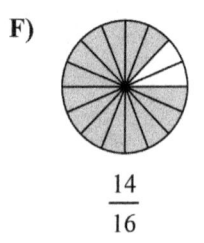

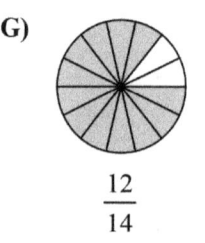

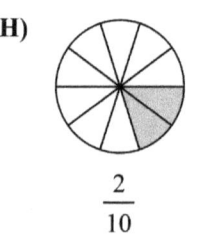

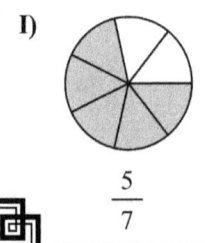

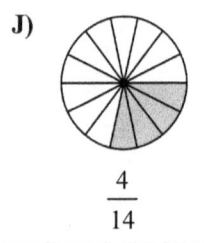

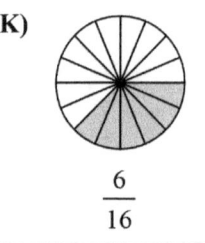

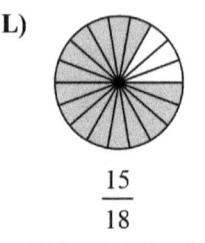

1)

$\dfrac{1}{6}$

2)

$\dfrac{3}{7}$

3)

$\dfrac{3}{8}$

4)

$\dfrac{2}{7}$

5)

$\dfrac{5}{20}$

6)

$\dfrac{7}{8}$

7)

$\dfrac{2}{14}$

8)

$\dfrac{10}{14}$

9)

$\dfrac{1}{5}$

10)

$\dfrac{6}{7}$

11)

$\dfrac{5}{6}$

12)

$\dfrac{3}{5}$

1. _____

2. _____

3. _____

4. _____

5. _____

6. _____

7. _____

8. _____

9. _____

10. _____

11. _____

12. _____

A)

$\dfrac{12}{20}$

B)

$\dfrac{3}{18}$

C)

$\dfrac{1}{4}$

D)

$\dfrac{6}{14}$

E)

$\dfrac{1}{7}$

F)

$\dfrac{14}{16}$

G)

$\dfrac{12}{14}$

H)

$\dfrac{2}{10}$

I)

$\dfrac{5}{7}$

J)

$\dfrac{4}{14}$

K)

$\dfrac{6}{16}$

L)

$\dfrac{15}{18}$

1)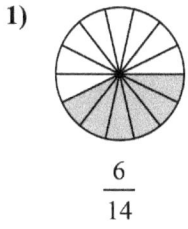

$\frac{6}{14}$

2)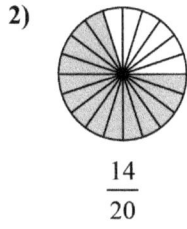

$\frac{14}{20}$

3)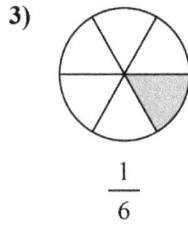

$\frac{1}{6}$

4)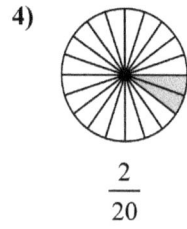

$\frac{2}{20}$

5)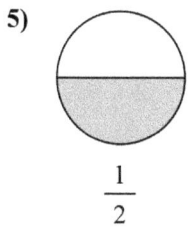

$\frac{1}{2}$

6)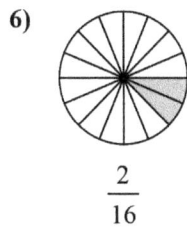

$\frac{2}{16}$

7)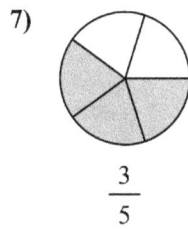

$\frac{3}{5}$

8)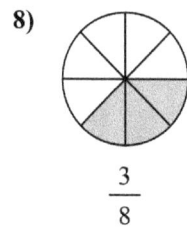

$\frac{3}{8}$

9)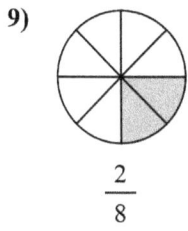

$\frac{2}{8}$

10)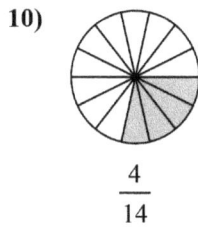

$\frac{4}{14}$

11)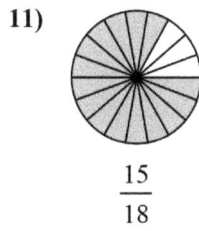

$\frac{15}{18}$

12)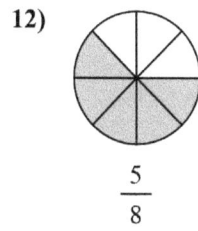

$\frac{5}{8}$

A)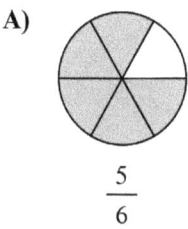

$\frac{5}{6}$

B)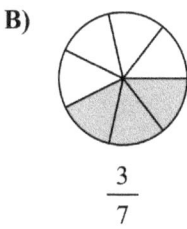

$\frac{3}{7}$

C)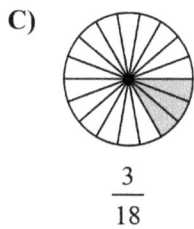

$\frac{3}{18}$

D)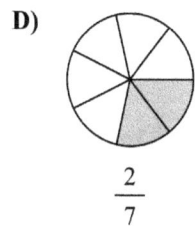

$\frac{2}{7}$

E)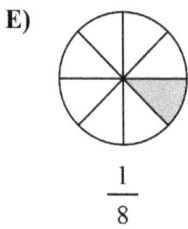

$\frac{1}{8}$

F)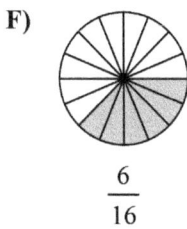

$\frac{6}{16}$

G)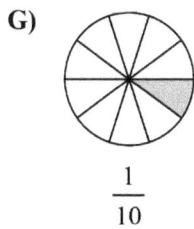

$\frac{1}{10}$

H)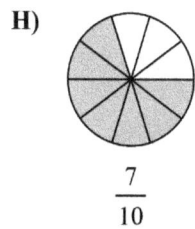

$\frac{7}{10}$

I)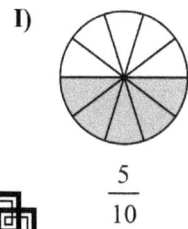

$\frac{5}{10}$

J)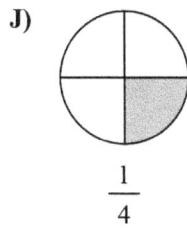

$\frac{1}{4}$

K)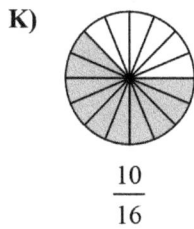

$\frac{10}{16}$

L)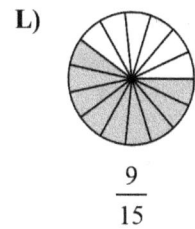

$\frac{9}{15}$

1. _____

2. _____

3. _____

4. _____

5. _____

6. _____

7. _____

8. _____

9. _____

10. _____

11. _____

12. _____

ANSWER KEY

1

1. $\dfrac{2}{8}$
2. $\dfrac{1}{3}$
3. $\dfrac{4}{8}$
4. $\dfrac{5}{6}$
5. $\dfrac{2}{4}$
6. $\dfrac{2}{6}$
7. $\dfrac{3}{4}$
8. $\dfrac{4}{6}$
9. $\dfrac{7}{8}$
10. $\dfrac{3}{8}$

2

1. $\dfrac{5}{6}$
2. $\dfrac{2}{4}$
3. $\dfrac{2}{6}$
4. $\dfrac{1}{6}$
5. $\dfrac{3}{4}$
6. $\dfrac{1}{4}$
7. $\dfrac{6}{8}$
8. $\dfrac{2}{8}$
9. $\dfrac{3}{8}$
10. $\dfrac{1}{3}$

3

1. $\dfrac{1}{4}$
2. $\dfrac{1}{3}$
3. $\dfrac{3}{4}$
4. $\dfrac{1}{2}$
5. $\dfrac{2}{8}$
6. $\dfrac{3}{6}$
7. $\dfrac{2}{6}$
8. $\dfrac{1}{6}$
9. $\dfrac{1}{8}$
10. $\dfrac{3}{8}$

4

1. $\dfrac{1}{2}$
2. $\dfrac{5}{6}$
3. $\dfrac{2}{4}$
4. $\dfrac{1}{8}$
5. $\dfrac{1}{4}$
6. $\dfrac{6}{8}$
7. $\dfrac{3}{8}$
8. $\dfrac{2}{3}$
9. $\dfrac{4}{6}$
10. $\dfrac{7}{8}$

5

1. _____ 2/8
2. _____ 3/4
3. _____ 3/8
4. _____ 5/6
5. _____ 1/3
6. _____ 7/8
7. _____ 4/8
8. _____ 2/6
9. _____ 4/6
10. _____ 6/8

6

1. _____ 3/8
2. _____ 3/4
3. _____ 1/8
4. _____ 2/3
5. _____ 1/2
6. _____ 4/6
7. _____ 4/8
8. _____ 3/6
9. _____ 2/4
10. _____ 1/3

7

1. _____ 7/8
2. _____ 3/6
3. _____ 4/8
4. _____ 1/4
5. _____ 5/6
6. _____ 3/8
7. _____ 2/4
8. _____ 1/3
9. _____ 5/8
10. _____ 2/6

8

1. _____ 4/6
2. _____ 2/4
3. _____ 5/8
4. _____ 2/3
5. _____ 3/8
6. _____ 1/2
7. _____ 2/6
8. _____ 5/6
9. _____ 1/3
10. _____ 1/6

9

1. _____ $\frac{4}{8}$ _____
2. _____ $\frac{3}{8}$ _____
3. _____ $\frac{5}{8}$ _____
4. _____ $\frac{2}{6}$ _____
5. _____ $\frac{1}{8}$ _____
6. _____ $\frac{1}{6}$ _____
7. _____ $\frac{4}{6}$ _____
8. _____ $\frac{1}{3}$ _____
9. _____ $\frac{6}{8}$ _____
10. _____ $\frac{5}{6}$ _____

10

1. _____ $\frac{2}{4}$ _____
2. _____ $\frac{3}{8}$ _____
3. _____ $\frac{1}{8}$ _____
4. _____ $\frac{1}{4}$ _____
5. _____ $\frac{1}{3}$ _____
6. _____ $\frac{1}{2}$ _____
7. _____ $\frac{3}{4}$ _____
8. _____ $\frac{5}{6}$ _____
9. _____ $\frac{6}{8}$ _____
10. _____ $\frac{3}{6}$ _____

11

1. _____ A,B,D _____
2. _____ D _____
3. _____ B _____
4. _____ B,D _____
5. _____ B,C _____
6. _____ A _____
7. _____ B,C _____
8. _____ A,B,C,D _____

12

1. _____ A,B,C,D _____
2. _____ A _____
3. _____ B _____
4. _____ A,B _____
5. _____ B,C _____
6. _____ A,B,C _____
7. _____ A,B,D _____
8. _____ A,B,C,D _____

13

1. none
2. B,C,D
3. C,D
4. A,D
5. none
6. B
7. none
8. A

14

1. A,B,D
2. B,C,D
3. A
4. B,C,D
5. D
6. A,B,C,D
7. A
8. A,B,C,D

15

1. B
2. A,B,C,D
3. A,B
4. A,B,C,D
5. A,B,C,D
6. A,B,C
7. none
8. B,D

16

1. B,C
2. none
3. A,C,D
4. A,B,C,D
5. B,C
6. A,B,C,D
7. A,C
8. B,D

17

1. A,B,C
2. A,B,C,D
3. B,C,D
4. none
5. A,B,C,D
6. A,B,C,D
7. none
8. none

18

1. A,B,D
2. none
3. none
4. A,B,D
5. C,D
6. A,B,C,D
7. A,C,D
8. D

19

1. A,B,C,D
2. A,C,D
3. A
4. C
5. A,C
6. A,B,D
7. C
8. B,C,D

20

1. A,B,C
2. A,B
3. A
4. B,C
5. A,D
6. A,B,C
7. B,D
8. D

21

1. $\frac{3}{8} + \frac{2}{8} = \frac{5}{8}$

2. $\frac{3}{10} + \frac{5}{10} = \frac{8}{10}$

3. $\frac{2}{8} + \frac{1}{8} = \frac{3}{8}$

4. $\frac{2}{5} + \frac{2}{5} = \frac{4}{5}$

5. $\frac{2}{6} + \frac{1}{6} = \frac{3}{6}$

6. $\frac{4}{10} + \frac{5}{10} = \frac{9}{10}$

7. $\frac{3}{6} + \frac{1}{6} = \frac{4}{6}$

8. $\frac{3}{8} + \frac{4}{8} = \frac{7}{8}$

9. $\frac{1}{6} + \frac{4}{6} = \frac{5}{6}$

10. $\frac{4}{12} + \frac{1}{12} = \frac{5}{12}$

22

1. $\frac{3}{4} + \frac{1}{4} = \frac{4}{4}$

2. $\frac{2}{5} + \frac{1}{5} = \frac{3}{5}$

3. $\frac{4}{6} + \frac{1}{6} = \frac{5}{6}$

4. $\frac{3}{8} + \frac{1}{8} = \frac{4}{8}$

5. $\frac{2}{4} + \frac{1}{4} = \frac{3}{4}$

6. $\frac{3}{10} + \frac{2}{10} = \frac{5}{10}$

7. $\frac{4}{8} + \frac{2}{8} = \frac{6}{8}$

8. $\frac{1}{5} + \frac{3}{5} = \frac{4}{5}$

9. $\frac{7}{10} + \frac{2}{10} = \frac{9}{10}$

10. $\frac{1}{3} + \frac{1}{3} = \frac{2}{3}$

23

1. $\frac{2}{4} + \frac{2}{4} = \frac{4}{4}$

2. $\frac{5}{12} + \frac{5}{12} = \frac{10}{12}$

3. $\frac{6}{10} + \frac{3}{10} = \frac{9}{10}$

4. $\frac{2}{6} + \frac{2}{6} = \frac{4}{6}$

5. $\frac{4}{6} + \frac{1}{6} = \frac{5}{6}$

6. $\frac{1}{5} + \frac{1}{5} = \frac{2}{5}$

7. $\frac{2}{12} + \frac{6}{12} = \frac{8}{12}$

8. $\frac{1}{3} + \frac{1}{3} = \frac{2}{3}$

9. $\frac{2}{8} + \frac{1}{8} = \frac{3}{8}$

10. $\frac{4}{8} + \frac{1}{8} = \frac{5}{8}$

24

1. $\frac{2}{4} + \frac{1}{4} = \frac{3}{4}$

2. $\frac{7}{12} + \frac{1}{12} = \frac{8}{12}$

3. $\frac{2}{10} + \frac{3}{10} = \frac{5}{10}$

4. $\frac{1}{5} + \frac{1}{5} = \frac{2}{5}$

5. $\frac{2}{5} + \frac{2}{5} = \frac{4}{5}$

6. $\frac{1}{4} + \frac{1}{4} = \frac{2}{4}$

7. $\frac{1}{8} + \frac{3}{8} = \frac{4}{8}$

8. $\frac{1}{6} + \frac{4}{6} = \frac{5}{6}$

9. $\frac{4}{12} + \frac{6}{12} = \frac{10}{12}$

10. $\frac{2}{12} + \frac{7}{12} = \frac{9}{12}$

25

1. $\frac{4}{8} + \frac{2}{8} = \frac{6}{8}$
2. $\frac{3}{6} + \frac{2}{6} = \frac{5}{6}$
3. $\frac{2}{4} + \frac{1}{4} = \frac{3}{4}$
4. $\frac{2}{5} + \frac{2}{5} = \frac{4}{5}$
5. $\frac{2}{5} + \frac{1}{5} = \frac{3}{5}$
6. $\frac{1}{8} + \frac{2}{8} = \frac{3}{8}$
7. $\frac{1}{4} + \frac{1}{4} = \frac{2}{4}$
8. $\frac{1}{3} + \frac{1}{3} = \frac{2}{3}$
9. $\frac{6}{10} + \frac{3}{10} = \frac{9}{10}$
10. $\frac{10}{12} + \frac{1}{12} = \frac{11}{12}$

26

1. $\frac{6}{12} + \frac{2}{12} = \frac{8}{12}$
2. $\frac{3}{8} + \frac{3}{8} = \frac{6}{8}$
3. $\frac{2}{4} + \frac{1}{4} = \frac{3}{4}$
4. $\frac{1}{5} + \frac{2}{5} = \frac{3}{5}$
5. $\frac{4}{10} + \frac{2}{10} = \frac{6}{10}$
6. $\frac{2}{5} + \frac{2}{5} = \frac{4}{5}$
7. $\frac{4}{6} + \frac{1}{6} = \frac{5}{6}$
8. $\frac{2}{12} + \frac{5}{12} = \frac{7}{12}$
9. $\frac{1}{4} + \frac{1}{4} = \frac{2}{4}$
10. $\frac{1}{6} + \frac{3}{6} = \frac{4}{6}$

27

1. $\frac{9}{12} + \frac{2}{12} = \frac{11}{12}$
2. $\frac{3}{5} + \frac{1}{5} = \frac{4}{5}$
3. $\frac{1}{6} + \frac{3}{6} = \frac{4}{6}$
4. $\frac{4}{6} + \frac{1}{6} = \frac{5}{6}$
5. $\frac{8}{12} + \frac{1}{12} = \frac{9}{12}$
6. $\frac{5}{12} + \frac{1}{12} = \frac{6}{12}$
7. $\frac{1}{6} + \frac{1}{6} = \frac{2}{6}$
8. $\frac{2}{10} + \frac{3}{10} = \frac{5}{10}$
9. $\frac{2}{8} + \frac{5}{8} = \frac{7}{8}$
10. $\frac{1}{5} + \frac{1}{5} = \frac{2}{5}$

28

1. $\frac{1}{5} + \frac{2}{5} = \frac{3}{5}$
2. $\frac{1}{6} + \frac{2}{6} = \frac{3}{6}$
3. $\frac{5}{12} + \frac{3}{12} = \frac{8}{12}$
4. $\frac{6}{10} + \frac{1}{10} = \frac{7}{10}$
5. $\frac{1}{6} + \frac{3}{6} = \frac{4}{6}$
6. $\frac{3}{12} + \frac{1}{12} = \frac{4}{12}$
7. $\frac{4}{8} + \frac{3}{8} = \frac{7}{8}$
8. $\frac{5}{8} + \frac{1}{8} = \frac{6}{8}$
9. $\frac{1}{4} + \frac{1}{4} = \frac{2}{4}$
10. $\frac{4}{6} + \frac{1}{6} = \frac{5}{6}$

29

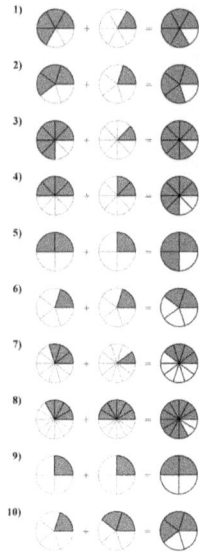

1. $\dfrac{4}{6} + \dfrac{1}{6} = \dfrac{5}{6}$

2. $\dfrac{3}{5} + \dfrac{1}{5} = \dfrac{4}{5}$

3. $\dfrac{6}{8} + \dfrac{1}{8} = \dfrac{7}{8}$

4. $\dfrac{4}{8} + \dfrac{2}{8} = \dfrac{6}{8}$

5. $\dfrac{2}{4} + \dfrac{1}{4} = \dfrac{3}{4}$

6. $\dfrac{1}{5} + \dfrac{1}{5} = \dfrac{2}{5}$

7. $\dfrac{3}{10} + \dfrac{1}{10} = \dfrac{4}{10}$

8. $\dfrac{4}{12} + \dfrac{6}{12} = \dfrac{10}{12}$

9. $\dfrac{1}{4} + \dfrac{1}{4} = \dfrac{2}{4}$

10. $\dfrac{1}{5} + \dfrac{2}{5} = \dfrac{3}{5}$

30

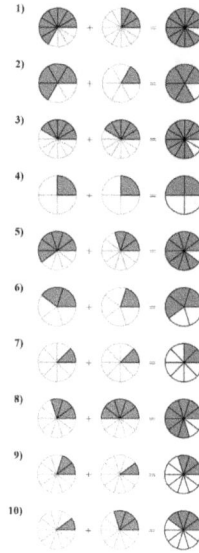

1. $\dfrac{8}{12} + \dfrac{3}{12} = \dfrac{11}{12}$

2. $\dfrac{4}{6} + \dfrac{1}{6} = \dfrac{5}{6}$

3. $\dfrac{5}{12} + \dfrac{5}{12} = \dfrac{10}{12}$

4. $\dfrac{1}{4} + \dfrac{1}{4} = \dfrac{2}{4}$

5. $\dfrac{6}{10} + \dfrac{3}{10} = \dfrac{9}{10}$

6. $\dfrac{2}{5} + \dfrac{1}{5} = \dfrac{3}{5}$

7. $\dfrac{1}{8} + \dfrac{1}{8} = \dfrac{2}{8}$

8. $\dfrac{3}{10} + \dfrac{5}{10} = \dfrac{8}{10}$

9. $\dfrac{2}{10} + \dfrac{1}{10} = \dfrac{3}{10}$

10. $\dfrac{1}{10} + \dfrac{3}{10} = \dfrac{4}{10}$

31

1) $\frac{1}{2} \times 7 =$ 2) $\frac{1}{3} \times 2 =$

3) $\frac{1}{3} \times 5 =$ 4) $\frac{1}{2} \times 5 =$

5) $\frac{3}{4} \times 4 =$ 6) $\frac{1}{4} \times 7 =$

7) $\frac{2}{6} \times 3 =$ 8) $\frac{1}{2} \times 5 =$

9) $\frac{1}{2} \times 5 =$ 10) $\frac{1}{3} \times 5 =$

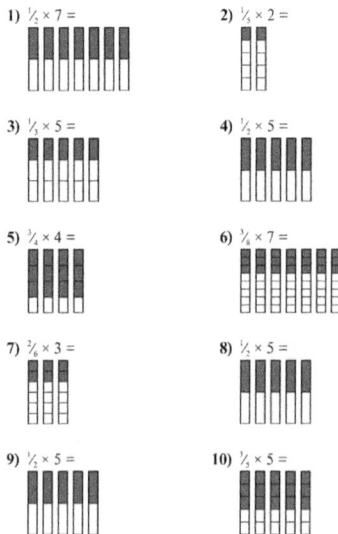

1. $\dfrac{7}{2}$

2. $\dfrac{2}{5}$

3. $\dfrac{5}{3}$

4. $\dfrac{5}{2}$

5. $\dfrac{12}{4}$

6. $\dfrac{21}{8}$

7. $\dfrac{6}{6}$

8. $\dfrac{5}{2}$

9. $\dfrac{5}{2}$

10. $\dfrac{15}{5}$

32

1) $\frac{1}{4} \times 9 =$ 2) $\frac{1}{4} \times 7 =$

3) $\frac{1}{3} \times 6 =$ 4) $\frac{9}{10} \times 2 =$

5) $\frac{1}{5} \times 4 =$ 6) $\frac{3}{4} \times 8 =$

7) $\frac{1}{2} \times 8 =$ 8) $\frac{3}{4} \times 4 =$

9) $\frac{2}{4} \times 2 =$ 10) $\frac{6}{8} \times 2 =$

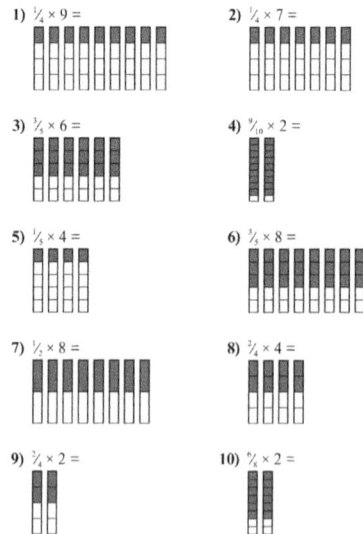

1. $\dfrac{9}{4}$

2. $\dfrac{7}{4}$

3. $\dfrac{18}{5}$

4. $\dfrac{18}{10}$

5. $\dfrac{4}{5}$

6. $\dfrac{24}{5}$

7. $\dfrac{8}{2}$

8. $\dfrac{8}{4}$

9. $\dfrac{4}{4}$

10. $\dfrac{12}{8}$

33

1) $\frac{9}{10} \times 6 =$

2) $\frac{7}{8} \times 7 =$

3) $\frac{2}{3} \times 4 =$

4) $\frac{5}{8} \times 5 =$

5) $\frac{2}{3} \times 5 =$

6) $\frac{1}{4} \times 5 =$

7) $\frac{9}{10} \times 8 =$

8) $\frac{2}{8} \times 9 =$

9) $\frac{1}{3} \times 4 =$

10) $\frac{2}{4} \times 7 =$

1. $\dfrac{54}{10}$
2. $\dfrac{49}{8}$
3. $\dfrac{8}{3}$
4. $\dfrac{25}{6}$
5. $\dfrac{10}{3}$
6. $\dfrac{5}{8}$
7. $\dfrac{72}{10}$
8. $\dfrac{18}{8}$
9. $\dfrac{12}{5}$
10. $\dfrac{14}{4}$

34

1) $\frac{2}{3} \times 9 =$

2) $\frac{7}{10} \times 7 =$

3) $\frac{6}{10} \times 2 =$

4) $\frac{2}{3} \times 7 =$

5) $\frac{1}{3} \times 5 =$

6) $\frac{2}{8} \times 7 =$

7) $\frac{2}{3} \times 9 =$

8) $\frac{1}{3} \times 3 =$

9) $\frac{1}{2} \times 5 =$

10) $\frac{3}{4} \times 9 =$

1. $\dfrac{18}{3}$
2. $\dfrac{49}{10}$
3. $\dfrac{12}{10}$
4. $\dfrac{14}{3}$
5. $\dfrac{5}{3}$
6. $\dfrac{14}{8}$
7. $\dfrac{18}{5}$
8. $\dfrac{3}{3}$
9. $\dfrac{5}{2}$
10. $\dfrac{27}{4}$

35

1) $\frac{1}{4} \times 7 =$

2) $\frac{6}{8} \times 9 =$

3) $\frac{1}{4} \times 3 =$

4) $\frac{2}{6} \times 9 =$

5) $\frac{1}{2} \times 9 =$

6) $\frac{1}{3} \times 6 =$

7) $\frac{1}{8} \times 3 =$

8) $\frac{2}{5} \times 5 =$

9) $\frac{1}{6} \times 4 =$

10) $\frac{1}{2} \times 6 =$

1. $\dfrac{7}{4}$
2. $\dfrac{54}{8}$
3. $\dfrac{21}{8}$
4. $\dfrac{18}{6}$
5. $\dfrac{9}{2}$
6. $\dfrac{6}{3}$
7. $\dfrac{3}{8}$
8. $\dfrac{10}{5}$
9. $\dfrac{20}{6}$
10. $\dfrac{6}{2}$

36

1) $\frac{5}{6} \times 5 =$

2) $\frac{2}{6} \times 8 =$

3) $\frac{5}{6} \times 5 =$

4) $\frac{1}{2} \times 6 =$

5) $\frac{2}{6} \times 9 =$

6) $\frac{2}{3} \times 3 =$

7) $\frac{2}{3} \times 5 =$

8) $\frac{1}{4} \times 3 =$

9) $\frac{5}{10} \times 3 =$

10) $\frac{3}{6} \times 8 =$

1. $\dfrac{25}{6}$
2. $\dfrac{16}{6}$
3. $\dfrac{25}{6}$
4. $\dfrac{6}{2}$
5. $\dfrac{18}{6}$
6. $\dfrac{6}{3}$
7. $\dfrac{10}{3}$
8. $\dfrac{9}{4}$
9. $\dfrac{15}{10}$
10. $\dfrac{24}{6}$

37

1) $\frac{1}{2} \times 4 =$

2) $\frac{1}{4} \times 8 =$

3) $\frac{7}{8} \times 8 =$

4) $\frac{6}{10} \times 5 =$

5) $\frac{2}{3} \times 3 =$

6) $\frac{6}{8} \times 5 =$

7) $\frac{5}{8} \times 4 =$

8) $\frac{1}{3} \times 8 =$

9) $\frac{3}{8} \times 8 =$

10) $\frac{6}{8} \times 7 =$

1. $\dfrac{4}{2}$

2. $\dfrac{8}{5}$

3. $\dfrac{56}{8}$

4. $\dfrac{30}{10}$

5. $\dfrac{6}{3}$

6. $\dfrac{30}{8}$

7. $\dfrac{20}{8}$

8. $\dfrac{8}{3}$

9. $\dfrac{24}{8}$

10. $\dfrac{42}{8}$

38

1) $\frac{1}{10} \times 9 =$

2) $\frac{3}{10} \times 6 =$

3) $\frac{2}{3} \times 4 =$

4) $\frac{1}{4} \times 8 =$

5) $\frac{3}{4} \times 9 =$

6) $\frac{1}{3} \times 3 =$

7) $\frac{1}{3} \times 7 =$

8) $\frac{3}{10} \times 3 =$

9) $\frac{3}{8} \times 8 =$

10) $\frac{1}{2} \times 5 =$

1. $\dfrac{9}{10}$

2. $\dfrac{18}{10}$

3. $\dfrac{12}{5}$

4. $\dfrac{32}{6}$

5. $\dfrac{27}{4}$

6. $\dfrac{9}{5}$

7. $\dfrac{7}{3}$

8. $\dfrac{9}{10}$

9. $\dfrac{24}{6}$

10. $\dfrac{5}{2}$

39

1) $\frac{4}{6} \times 9 =$

2) $\frac{2}{10} \times 2 =$

3) $\frac{1}{4} \times 4 =$

4) $\frac{4}{8} \times 4 =$

5) $\frac{1}{2} \times 7 =$

6) $\frac{1}{2} \times 2 =$

7) $\frac{2}{4} \times 6 =$

8) $\frac{2}{3} \times 8 =$

9) $\frac{2}{4} \times 8 =$

10) $\frac{4}{6} \times 6 =$

1. $\dfrac{36}{6}$

2. $\dfrac{4}{10}$

3. $\dfrac{16}{8}$

4. $\dfrac{16}{8}$

5. $\dfrac{7}{2}$

6. $\dfrac{2}{2}$

7. $\dfrac{12}{4}$

8. $\dfrac{16}{3}$

9. $\dfrac{16}{4}$

10. $\dfrac{24}{6}$

40

1) $\frac{1}{5} \times 3 =$

2) $\frac{2}{4} \times 9 =$

3) $\frac{3}{4} \times 4 =$

4) $\frac{3}{4} \times 3 =$

5) $\frac{2}{3} \times 3 =$

6) $\frac{1}{2} \times 3 =$

7) $\frac{1}{6} \times 7 =$

8) $\frac{3}{4} \times 6 =$

9) $\frac{3}{8} \times 3 =$

10) $\frac{1}{8} \times 5 =$

1. $\dfrac{3}{5}$

2. $\dfrac{18}{8}$

3. $\dfrac{12}{4}$

4. $\dfrac{6}{4}$

5. $\dfrac{6}{3}$

6. $\dfrac{3}{2}$

7. $\dfrac{7}{6}$

8. $\dfrac{18}{4}$

9. $\dfrac{9}{8}$

10. $\dfrac{25}{8}$

41

1. $\frac{4}{8}$
2. $\frac{2}{8}$
3. $\frac{3}{8}$
4. $\frac{3}{6}$
5. $\frac{1}{3}$
6. $\frac{6}{8}$
7. $\frac{2}{6}$
8. $\frac{1}{4}$
9. $\frac{3}{8}$
10. $\frac{1}{3}$

42

1. $\frac{1}{6}$
2. $\frac{6}{8}$
3. $\frac{3}{6}$
4. $\frac{5}{8}$
5. $\frac{5}{8}$
6. $\frac{1}{3}$
7. $\frac{2}{3}$
8. $\frac{5}{8}$
9. $\frac{3}{6}$
10. $\frac{3}{8}$

43

1. $\frac{2}{6}$
2. $\frac{1}{6}$
3. $\frac{1}{3}$
4. $\frac{3}{4}$
5. $\frac{3}{8}$
6. $\frac{2}{3}$
7. $\frac{1}{2}$
8. $\frac{2}{8}$
9. $\frac{3}{8}$
10. $\frac{3}{6}$

44

1. $\frac{2}{3}$
2. $\frac{1}{2}$
3. $\frac{1}{3}$
4. $\frac{2}{6}$
5. $\frac{2}{3}$
6. $\frac{3}{6}$
7. $\frac{1}{4}$
8. $\frac{1}{2}$
9. $\frac{3}{4}$
10. $\frac{1}{4}$

45

1. $\frac{2}{8}$
2. $\frac{3}{4}$
3. $\frac{2}{3}$
4. $\frac{2}{6}$
5. $\frac{3}{6}$
6. $\frac{5}{8}$
7. $\frac{1}{6}$
8. $\frac{2}{3}$
9. $\frac{1}{6}$
10. $\frac{5}{8}$

46

1. $\frac{2}{4}$
2. $\frac{5}{8}$
3. $\frac{2}{8}$
4. $\frac{3}{4}$
5. $\frac{3}{8}$
6. $\frac{2}{3}$
7. $\frac{4}{8}$
8. $\frac{4}{8}$
9. $\frac{2}{6}$
10. $\frac{1}{6}$

47

1. $\frac{3}{8}$
2. $\frac{2}{4}$
3. $\frac{1}{4}$
4. $\frac{3}{8}$
5. $\frac{1}{6}$
6. $\frac{3}{4}$
7. $\frac{3}{8}$
8. $\frac{3}{8}$
9. $\frac{3}{6}$
10. $\frac{1}{3}$

48

1. $\frac{3}{4}$
2. $\frac{3}{8}$
3. $\frac{3}{8}$
4. $\frac{2}{6}$
5. $\frac{2}{4}$
6. $\frac{2}{6}$
7. $\frac{3}{6}$
8. $\frac{1}{3}$
9. $\frac{4}{8}$
10. $\frac{2}{3}$

49

1. $\frac{5}{8}$
2. $\frac{1}{2}$
3. $\frac{6}{8}$
4. $\frac{6}{8}$
5. $\frac{1}{3}$
6. $\frac{1}{6}$
7. $\frac{3}{4}$
8. $\frac{1}{2}$
9. $\frac{2}{3}$
10. $\frac{5}{8}$

50

1. $\frac{5}{8}$
2. $\frac{3}{8}$
3. $\frac{5}{8}$
4. $\frac{2}{4}$
5. $\frac{3}{4}$
6. $\frac{2}{3}$
7. $\frac{3}{8}$
8. $\frac{2}{3}$
9. $\frac{4}{6}$
10. $\frac{1}{4}$

51

1. I
2. A
3. B
4. C
5. F
6. K
7. E
8. G
9. D
10. H
11. J
12. L

52

1. E
2. A
3. I
4. J
5. F
6. D
7. G
8. C
9. B
10. L
11. H
12. K

53

1. D
2. F
3. I
4. K
5. A
6. B
7. L
8. J
9. C
10. H
11. E
12. G

54

1. L
2. A
3. K
4. J
5. B
6. D
7. G
8. C
9. I
10. F
11. E
12. H

55

1. J
2. I
3. A
4. L
5. K
6. H
7. G
8. C
9. D
10. F
11. B
12. E

56

1. C
2. J
3. A
4. G
5. L
6. B
7. F
8. D
9. K
10. I
11. E
12. H

57

1. F
2. I
3. D
4. G
5. J
6. K
7. C
8. L
9. A
10. B
11. E
12. H

58

1. F
2. C
3. A
4. J
5. I
6. H
7. E
8. G
9. B
10. D
11. L
12. K

59

1. B
2. D
3. K
4. J
5. C
6. F
7. E
8. I
9. H
10. G
11. L
12. A

60

1. B
2. H
3. C
4. G
5. I
6. E
7. L
8. F
9. J
10. D
11. A
12. K